BURMA-SHAVE

The Rhymes, the Signs, the Times

Bill Vossler

NORTH STAR PRESS OF ST. CLOUD, INC.

Cover Photo: Nikki Rajala

Second Printing, January 1998
Third Printing, June 1998
Fourth Printing, October 1998
Fifth Printing, April 1999
Sixth Printing, August 1999
Seventh Printing, March 2000
Eighth Printing, January 2001
Ninth Printing, December 2001
Tenth Printing, March 2002
Eleventh Printing, August 2002
Twelfth Printing, September 2003
Thirteenth Printing, May 2004
ISBN: 0-87839-122-3

Printed in the United States of America by
Versa Press, Inc., East Peoria, Illinois.

Published by
North Star Press of St. Cloud, Inc.
P.O. Box 451
St. Cloud, Minnesota 56302

Dedicated to my wife
Nikki
inspiration for this book
&
joy of my life

PREFACE

American writer Alexander Woollcott wrote that like eating salted peanuts, nobody could read just one Burma-Shave sign. He may have been right.

This book is crammed full of peanuts, all the different Burma-Shave rhymes you have come to know and love. What's better, you can find any rhyme without wading through all 556 of them, simply by using the handy Burma-Shave rhyme index at the back of the book.

Choose a key word from any Burma-Shave rhyme, and you will be able to find the rhyme. So if you know but one key word, like "skinless":

> He lit a match
> To check gas tank
> That's why
> They call him
> Skinless Frank
> Burma-Shave. (Verse 1)

just look up "skinless" in the Burma-Shave rhyme index, and then find the numbered rhyme it refers to. (In this case, Verse 1). Verse 1 could also be found through other key words: match, check, gas, tank, and Frank. Thus you can find any verse quickly and easily. The verses are numbered chronologically, from first to last in the pages of the book, and those not used in the text are listed separately in the last chapter.

Another example: if you wanted to find the exact words to a verse you remembered that contained "harps":

Road
Was slippery
Curve was sharp
White robe, halo
Wings and harp
Burma-Shave. (Verse 2)

Other key words for Verse 2 include road, slippery, curve, sharp, white, robe, halo, and wings.

Rhymes without numbers were not official Burma-Shave signs.

I am indebted to Grace Odell, Clinton B. Odell, and George Hamley Odell, for interviews with them, and for supplying me with information and photos. All photos in this book come from them except for ads and those otherwise identified. I am also indebted to Delaney Communications, Inc., of Cincinnati, Ohio, for their fine video, *The Signs and Rhymes of Burma-Shave*, which gives a visual history of the company, and to Roy Bernick, whose gorgeous 1929 Model A Ford graces the cover of this book. And also to Frank Rowsome, Jr., who got it all started with his little book, *The Verse by the Side of the Road*. When I read his book years ago, I read my first "peanut," and I haven't stopped since.

Anyone with additional information and photos about Burma-Shave, please contact me.

Bill Vossler
400 Caroline Lane
P.O. Box 372
Rockville, MN 56369
320-253-5414

TABLE OF CONTENTS

Chapter 1

BURMA-SHAVE
THE GOOD OLD DAYS

*D*uring the midst of the Cold War between the United States and Russia, shivering American sailors on the deck of a ship in the Bering Strait were astonished to round an iceberg and spot a heart-warming sight: a string of six small red signs planted in ice floes. The rhymed messages on the signs were about polar bears.

In Russian.

And the last sign said Burma-Shave.

The sailors soon discovered these Burma-Shave signs were a ruse perpetrated by their own reconnaissance helicopter, which was flying ahead of the ship, in an attempt to lighten up dreary days at sea.

Had those signs actually been Russian, few people would have been surprised. By the 1960s, Burma-Shave signs had found their way from Minnesota Highway 65 between Minneapolis and Albert Lea, (near what is Lakeville today), where they made their first appearance in 1925, to nearly everywhere around the world. Returning United States servicemen said they had seen them in all European war theatres, and some enterprising U.S. soldiers even put them up on the Burma trail as warm reminders of home.

Today Burma-Shave remains one of America's fondest-remembered products, especially by generations of Americans who grew up between 1925 and 1955, when the American automobile was growing up, as well as the country itself.

Burma-Shave signs even found their way to Antarctica, where they were erected by the United States Navy. It appears in this sign that the penguins are waiting for the girls. The entire set of signs read, "Use our cream and we betcha girls won't wait, they'll come and getcha. Burma-Shave."

In fact, if you say "Burma-Shave" in a group of mixed-age people, you will instantly be able to tell who matured along with Burma-Shave—their eyes will light up, and they will want to recite their favorite rhyme or two to you—while others will screw up their faces questioningly and say "Burma what?"

During the thirty-seven years the signs graced United States highways in forty-five states, the rhymes and the signs came to represent the best times of America—times when America was steeped in the good feelings of victories in two World Wars. Times when the American dream of rags to riches was more vivid and seemingly more reachable by everybody. (In fact, Burma-Vita was the very embodiment of the American dream, the company teetering on the brink of failure in 1925, and rising to pre-eminence in the field of shaving in the 1930s and later.) A time when a person's word and a handshake sealed a deal, and a person's word was bond. A time when the efforts of a generation working together could raise a stagnant nation out of the worst period of despair in its history, the Great Depression. In

In those days, America was a different place, and many believe it was better. (Photo courtesy of Stearns County Historical Society, St. Cloud, Minnesota)

short, Burma-Vita (the company that manufactured Burma-Shave) and Burma-Shave matured at a time when the world, in retrospective belief if not in reality, was a kinder, better and more honest place and time.

But Burma-Vita Company, and Burma-Shave, almost didn't make it.

A Great Idea, a Little Luck, and a Lot of Pluck

TURN-OF-THE-CENTURY LAWYERS had a difficult time making a living at lawyering. Many of them needed other sources of income. For Minneapolis lawyer Robert Ransom Odell, the founder of the Burma-Vita Company, one way to make money was manufacturing and selling a liniment.

"My grandfather," said Robert's grandson Leonard Odell, in Frank Rowsome Jr.'s *The Verse by the Side of the Road*, "was an attorney in the early days of Minneapolis. In those times lawyers were short on education and long on enterprise, and Grandfather had each of these attributes. For a time he was the U.S. marshal here, with the duty of apprehending men who sold liquor to the Indians. He claimed he'd procured the liniment recipe from an old sea captain, and perhaps he did. Of course, most all those liniments came from sea captains. They traveled the world and encountered witch doctors and collected secret potions. He made it there for many years, selling it through a couple of drugstores in lower Minneapolis."

3

Long before Burma-Shave even inkled of lathering faces, its antecedent product was called Burma-Vita (its camphor, cassia, and cajeput came from the Malay peninsula, where Burma is located, plus Latin *vita,* for "life"), and it was a liniment, not a shaving cream, and a rather foul-smelling liniment at that.

Leonard added, "Grandfather made the potion in his fifth-floor law office, but you could smell it everywhere, which probably didn't endear him to his fellow tenants."

Nor to his customers. Druggists gently suggested that maybe he would have more luck if he sold a regularly needed product, instead of one only used when they were sick.

By 1925, the company was in a lather. It was broke, its sales declining, and its product unknown. Robert Odell had been disabled by a stroke, and his son Clinton M. Odell, a very successful insurance salesman with White and Odell Agency, had been forced to resign because of health problems. Sciatica had put him on his back in bed for parts of several years.

Despite near destitution, Clinton sent twenty-five dollars to gravely-ill and down-and-out chemist Carl Noren, who had been forced to move to the desert for his health.

Burma-Vita Company, which then included Robert's son Clinton, and Clinton's sons Allan and Leonard, was failing. With Burma-Vita sales practically nonexistent, Clinton had been toying with the idea of a new and revolutionary product: a brushless shaving cream.

As a veteran traveling salesman, he had often suffered the indignities of shaving brushes reeking of mildew and foul smells after being stored wet in his dop kit during constant travel. Clinton saw the advantage of a brushless shaving cream.

That's when Carl Noren reappeared. Noren, like Clinton M. Odell, had regained his health, and asked if he could do anything to repay the earlier kindness shown to him. Clinton tossed him a tube of a British brushless shaving cream called Lloyd's Euxgesis, and asked Noren to make a better product.

Over the next few months, using Burma-Vita as a base, Noren concocted more than 300 different mixes but without success. But the story goes that one day a bottle of No. 143 (some say 153) was discovered languishing in the back of a shelf where it had aged for two months. It met all the conditions for a new brushless shaving cream.

Chapter 2

BEFORE THE SIGNS

urma-Shave shaving cream was not an automatic seller, and did not sell well its first year of 1925-1926. Add the Odells' unusual business methods, and many people would not have given it much chance of long-term survival. Rarely did the Odells approach business in the accepted ways.

Their methods were creative, however. One of their early advertising techniques, for instance, consisted of "Jars on Approval," where the Odells accosted perfect strangers on the street. ("Take it home, try it, and if you like it, pay me fifty cents next week.")

Though creative, it simply didn't work. As a result, sales for the first year were negligible.

Evelyn S. Dorman wrote in *Consumer Brands*, "Selling a new shaving cream—one that was brushless—required the changing of ingrained habits, so the Odells sold Burma-Shave on its convenience, speed, and modernity. The competition, however, was not far behind. Molle, Krank's Shaving Cream and Barbasol soon launched brushless shaving creams, followed by the Colgate-Palmolive and Williams companies."

Burma-Shave also tried direct sales in business places, as well as door-to-door sales, but with the same meager luck.

Until that one day when Allan was on the road trying to sell the shaving cream. On that 1925 day, he discovered the concept that would make Burma-Shave a household name.

The familiar jar of Burma-Shave was used first by Father for shaving, and then by Mother for canning.

Alongside a road between Aurora and Joliet, Illinois, he noticed a set of signs, each advertising a gasoline station further up the road. Sharon Carter wrote in *American History* magazine that each sign contained one word, like "Gas," "Oil," "Restrooms," and the last sign pointed to the service station itself. Carter said "Noticing the compulsion he felt to read each of the signs as they appeared, Allan wondered 'why can't you sell a product that way?'"

That was Allan's stroke of genius. Why not advertise Burma-Shave with a series of signs set by the side of the road? The car had just recently taken on new importance and meaning to average Americans, and had won their hearts; more and more people were taking to the roads, for business and for leisure. It seemed like the perfect concept. Until Allan asked his father, Clinton M. Odell, about the possibility of erecting similar sets of signs. Clinton checked with Chicago advertising experts, who were uniform in their disagreement: six signs by the side of the road wouldn't work. *Sales Management* magazine asked in an article whether a legitimate advertising campaign might not do better.

The original brain trust for Burma-Vita Company included Clinton M. Odell (seated), and his sons Leonard (left) and Allan (right). Allan came up with the idea for six signs by the side of the road.

Allan was undeterred; he felt in his bones that the signs would work. Finally he convinced his father to give him two hundred dollars of company money to give the concept a try.

Though money was tight, Clinton advanced the money. In September 1926, the Odells bought secondhand boards from Rose Brothers Wrecking Company in Minneapolis. In *The Verse by the Side of the Road*, Leonard Odell said "The boards had plenty of nailholes and some were burned on one side. We sawed them and painted them up, using a thin brass stencil and brush."

Before the ground froze, a dozen sets of signs were dug in alongside two roads out of Minneapolis, Highway 65 to Albert Lea and Highway 61 to Red Wing, Minnesota. They sported unrhymed jingles, which today seem very un-Burma-Shave-like:

> Shave
> The modern way
> Fine
> For the skin
> Druggists have it
> Burma-Shave. (Verse 3)

Winter set in, the families had little money, and if the company was not going to fold, it needed capital. So Clinton set forth, and used his old insurance skills to raise money.

Leonard Odell said in Delaney Communications, Inc., video, *The Signs and Rhymes of Burma-Shave*, that in three weeks his father did the greatest selling job ever. He took a busted company, with an idea that the experts said would never work, and a product that nobody believed in—brushless shaving cream—"and with those things going for him, he sold forty-nine percent of the stock, and raised money to incorporate, and start the company, and the sign shop." Burma-Vita Company was incorporated November 18, 1926.

Those first crude signs began to work, effective beyond anyone's wildest imaginings, never giving Clinton any reason to doubt his decision in investing in them.

By January 1927, the company was reaping its first repeat orders ever, from druggists serving travelers on the roads with the signs. Business skyrocketed from nothing to $68,000 in one year.

It had been a close shave; but Burma-Shave was saved.

Chapter 3

EARLY JINGLES

*T*he first 1927 Burma-Shave signs were very dull compared to later ones, and few remember that they were just simple advertisements:

Shave the modern way.
No brush, no lather
No rub-in.
Big tube 35 cents.
Drug stores.
Burma-Shave. (Verse 4)

Or 1928's

Take's the "H" out of shave
Makes it save
Saves complexion
Saves time & money
No brush, no lather
Burma-Shave. (Verse 5)

They worked as advertisements to fit on the six little signs by the side of the road, but the concept was in its infancy, and would not have met the later and higher standards of Burma-Shave rhymes and humor.

Some of these early ones were very wordy, as well:

Goodbye! shaving brush.
Half a pound for half a dollar.
Very fine for the skin.
Druggists have it.
Cheer up face. The war is over.
Burma-Shave. (Verse 6)

Or

One of the great discoveries.
Goodbye shaving brush.
Old men look younger.
Young men look handsomer.
Very fine for the skin.
Burma-Shave. (1928) (Verse 7)

But at least one of the verses, from 1928, presaged the humor and the rhymes that would eventually follow on Burma-Shave signs:

Holler.
Half a pound for half a dollar.
Oh boy!
Shaving joy!
Complexion save.
Burma-Shave. (Verse 8)

Perhaps the Odells got tired of using plain old advertisements on the signs—they built the Burma-Vita business listening to their own individual and creative voices—and in starting to create rhyme and humor also diverted from "normal" or "accepted" advertising practice. Whatever happened, by 1929 the familiar rhythm of the Burma-Shave signs had been established:

Every shaver
Now can snore
Six more minutes
Than before
By using
Burma-Shave. (Verse 9)

10

Allan was writing most of the jingles. Grace Odell, Allan's wife, said in *The Signs and Rhymes of Burma-Shave* that "Allan had the idea that [the rhymes were] something you could laugh at, and something so you wouldn't go to sleep when you were driving your car. He was always a dreamer, and had such wonderful thoughts."

When those thoughts did come into his mind, Grace was ready. She kept a flashlight, pad of paper, and a pen by the side of the bed. She never knew when he might wake her in the middle of the night and ask her to write one of the ditties down.

Grace said, "Allan would get his ideas in the middle of the night, any time from 3:00 to 5:00 in the morning. He would say, 'Grace, I've got one,' and I had to have a pencil and paper and a flashlight by my bed, because I couldn't even get up and put the light on because he would forget what he was going to tell me."

It might be:

> Your shaving brush
> Has had its day
> So why not
> Shave the modern way
> With
> Burma-Shave. (Verse 10)

"Many of those brainstorms," wrote Don Boxmeyer in the *Pioneer Press*, of St. Paul, Minnesota, on July 23, 1997, "wound up on the side of some country road, memorialized in little red-and-white six-part homilies filled with homespun wisdom that became a national philosophy for a simpler time:

> Shaving brushes
> You'll soon see 'em
> On the shelf
> In some
> Museum
> Burma-Shave. (Verse 11)

Grace said, "The next morning he'd ask, 'Did I say anything last night?' and I'd show him. Pretty soon, it would be another set of signs:"

No matter how
You slice it
It's still your face
Be humane
Use
Burma-Shave. (Verse 12)

Allan and his father (Clinton M. Odell) wrote all of the first signs until they ran dry. "Then, about the time friends observed that he was beginning to talk in Burma-Shave verse," Richard and Joan Dunlop wrote in "What Happened to the Burma-Shave Signs" in *Home & Away* magazine, "he announced an annual national contest for bards of the open road."

Grace added, "That's when the contest around the country took over. That's when all of these jingles came in."

Cheer up face
The war is past
The "H"is out
Of shave
At last
Burma-Shave. (Verse 13)

Chapter 4

IN 20 WORDS OR LESS . . .
THE CONTESTS

J ust as nobody anticipated the quick success of Burma-Shave, nobody anticipated the success of the Burma-Shave jingle contests, either. Success meant more advertising, and more jingles, and Allan Odell, primary creator of the jingles, was wearing out.

Thus he turned to his national audience for help. The first year the contest was held— about 1930—700 entries were submitted. A dozen were chosen. Eventually 65,000 submissions a year flooded in, many addressed to B. Billious Rangoon, Sales Manager, a pseudonym Allan had used in an

● It's BURMA SHAVE time again! From now until Tuesday, February 28, 1950, you have an opportunity to win one of 589 prizes, ranging from twenty prizes of $100 in cash to five hundred Gift Kits valued at $1.75. You are to write jingles worded to fit a series of six road-side signs, with the last line always "Burma Shave".

They want jingles on Safe Driving, Humor, Brushless, Economy, Tough Beards-Tender Skin, and Avoid Substitutes. Print your name and address and enclose a top or bottom flap from any size Burma Shave carton with each entry. (By allowing you to use either top or bottom as a qualifier—you get two tries with each carton.) Jingles will be judged on the basis of brevity, originality and interest. The address—Burma Shave Company, Dept. D, 2318 Chestnut Avenue, Minneapolis, 5, Minnesota.

ad in *New Yorker* magazine. Prizes were $100, and later upped to $1,000. On the average, twenty jingles were chosen per year.

Early submitted jingles were businesslike:

Shave the modern way
Wash the face
Apply with fingers
Shave
Big tube 35¢
Burma-Shave. (Verse 14)

But as years went by, more and more became humorous as in this 1930 rhyme:

Are your whiskers
When you wake
Tougher than a
Two-bit steak?
Try
Burma-Shave. (Verse 15)

Or, 1933's

He played a sax
Had no B.O.
But his whiskers
Scratched
So she let him go
Burma-Shave. (Verse 16)

Or this one from 1934:

When cutting
Whiskers
You don't need
To leave one half
Of them for seed
Burma-Shave. (Verse 17)

Burma-Shave advertised their contest everywhere, as the contest literature trumpeted: "The annual Burma-Shave 'Jingle Round-up' is now on. This contest is being publicized in Sunday supplements, such as 'This Week' and 'Parade,' as well as all contest magazines. As it takes a box top (any size) to qual-

After the success of Burma-Shave in the late 1920s, Burma-Vita needed an influx of new rhymes to fill all the signs that were being put in, and Allan Odell was running dry after years of thinking up rhymes. The result was the highly successful yearly Burma-Shave jingle contest.

ify each entry, be sure you have plenty of Burma-Shave available for your cus-tomers, many of whom will wish to enter this contest. Last year [1949] we received 52,020 entries to this contest. We expect more this year. See that the contestants buy their Burma-Shave from you so they can qualify. DON'T FAIL TO TAKE ADVANTAGE OF THE ABOVE BONUS DEALS. They mean money to you at a time when Burma-Shave is really 'on the move.'"

Other magazines in which Burma-Shave advertised included *American Legion* to *Contest Magazine* to *American Druggist* and a series of Army and Navy magazines, with heavy emphasis on the drugstore and drug-trade journals.

George Hamley Odell, Allan Odell's youngest son, said when he was growing up he remembers the family sessions discussing which jingles might be used on the signs. "Each family got a list of the jingles submitted for the contest, and we would rank them. Some were pretty raunchy and ended up being thrown away, which was real unfortunate, I think."

His older brother Clinton B. Odell also remembered the contests. "People would come up with all sorts of wild stuff, and my folks would make a list of the off-color ones. I remember as a child, I knew when they had a contest, because my mom and dad would go in the den and close the door, and there'd be this uproarious laughter, so I knew they'd had a contest. They had a lot of fun."

The contest was held yearly. The 1949 contest was headed EARN $100.00 OR MORE. WRITE ROAD SIGN JINGLES FOR BURMA-SHAVE! and offered 589 awards, from twenty prizes of $100 in cash, to fifty awards of two dollars each, and 500 consolation awards, "each consisting of a Burma-Shave Gift Kit [retail value $1.75] containing Burma-Shave, razor blades, after shave lotion, and talc."

The literature proclaimed: "You know those catchy Burma-Shave signs that stand six in a row along the highway. We need clever new jingles to use on them in 1950. We'll pay well for the jingles we accept. Send in as many jingles as you wish (enclosing the top or bottom of a Burma-Shave carton with each jingle.) You'll have a bushel of fun—and you might win several awards!"

Then the sheet gave specific directions on what to write about: "Jingles should be worded to fit a series of six signs, the last sign reading 'Burma-Shave.' Each jingle should rhyme.

16

JINGLES OF ALL THE FOLLOWING TYPES WILL BE USED:

A. Safe Driving. . . "A man who passes, On hills and curves, Is not a man, Of iron nerves, He's crazy! Burma-Shave." (Verse 18)
B. Humor. . . "With a sleek cheek, Pressed to hers, Jeepers! Creepers!! How she purrs. Burma-Shave." (Verse 19)
C. Brushless. . . "The more, You shave, The brushless way, The more you'll be, Inclined to say, Burma-Shave." (Verse 20)
D. Economy. . . "Thrifty jars for, Stay at homes, Handy tubes, For him, Who roams. Burma-Shave." (Verse 21)
E. Tough Beards, Tender Skin . . . "Said one whisker, To another, Can't get tough, With this stuff, Brother, Burma-Shave." (Verse 22)
F. Avoid Substitutes. . . "Substitutes and, Imitations, Send 'em to, Your wife's, Relations, Burma-Shave." (Verse 23)

The rules for the contest were as follows:

1. Send in as many jingles as you wish. (Send only your best ones, because quality is what counts.)
2. Send in with each jingle the top or bottom of any size Burma-Shave carton.
3. Print or type jingles, using only one side of paper. Set jingle in six lines (last line being "Burma-Shave.") Print your name and address on each sheet of paper used.
4. Jingles must be postmarked on or before February 28, 1949.
5. Jingles will be judged on brevity, originality, and interest. Judges' decision will be final. It will be impossible to carry on correspondence about the competition. No jingles can be returned, but every one used will be paid for.
6. Winners will be notified shortly after April 1, 1949. List of twenty top winners will be published in most contest magazines, or mailed to anyone who requests it, after April 1, 1949.
7. Mail your jingles to: Dept. D, Burma Shave Co., 2318 Chestnut Ave., Minneapolis 5, Minn.

Write a jingle, Send it in, Think of, The money, It may win! Burma-Shave."

Additional contests clarified what Burma-Vita people wanted for their jingle: "It should be easily and quickly understood and should carry a surprise punch if possible. Human interest is important. Cleverness and orig-inality are imperative. Brevity, of course, is a 'must.'"

Burma-Shave wasn't afraid to advertise in its own literature to push the contest: "Get yourself some Burma-Shave—in handy tube or economy jar—from your druggist. See how thoroughly Burma-Shave softens tough whiskers and soothes tender skin. Then get busy thinking up some choice Burma-Shave jingles."

In another contest, they added: "Be sure your jingles RHYME. 'Whiskers' does not rhyme with 'Misters'—although a lot of people would have us think these are 'rhyme' words."

The Funny Business

Contest magazines announced the yearly Burma-Shave jingle contests, and later, the winners: "Millie Berglund was flashing a $100 check from Burma-Shave, and the gal was thrilled beyond measure since she's attempted con-testing for some time and this was her first win."

During the same contest, a woman from Pennsylvania won in the Burma-Shave contest: "One of our gals got $25 from Burma-Shave, and Jo Bodle of Philly, is thrilled to pieces. Although Jo has won nice local prizes, this is her first national win and getting $100 and $2 from Burma-Shave is a nice way to start winning in nationals."

Three women and seven men, all with considerable contest judging experience, were chosen for preliminary judging of the jingles, while Burma-Vita officers made the final decisions. The 1950 jingle contest shows how widespread the use of Burma-Shave was, with winners that year from New Jersey to Ohio to Iowa to Minnesota to Texas to Utah and California.

Today, most contests don't allow employees to enter their compa-ny's competitions, if there is the least affiliation, but Burma-Vita didn't make a distinction, perhaps because the Odells themselves were honest, and couldn't imagine other people not being honest: "How many of you Druggists, and your customers will earn $100 or more on the BIG BURMA-SHAVE JINGLE CONTEST which is now being advertised throughout the nation?"

By the time 1952 rolled around, the contest literature said that too many jingles about humor and safe driving were being submitted. Burma-Vita said they'd rather have more about Burma-Shave being brushless, its economy, jingles on tough beards and tender skins, and not accepting substitutes.

In retrospect, that was probably a mistake. Burma-Shave entered the American consciousness through humor. That's what Americans liked most about the jingles. That's what separated Burma-Vita's advertising from the advertising of almost every other American company. When Burma-Shave lessened their emphasis on humor, they stepped back from what had made them different, had set them apart, and had made them successful. They faded back into the pack.

In defense of Burma-Vita, by 1952, business was not booming. Perhaps they figured a change in direction was needed, something to perk up the company's flat sales. In reality, perhaps there was nothing they could do. Perhaps Burma-Shave had simply run its course.

Shysters plied their trade even during those halcyon days, as an article in the *Gotham Gazette* newspaper said. A man wrote that an Ohioan had won some money in that year's Burma-Shave jingles contest, with this jingle:

If harmony
Is what
You crave
Then get
A tuba
Burma-Shave. (Verse 24)

The man wrote, "I don't understand how that could be, since this jingle happens to be the identical verse that won $100 for me fifteen years ago, in Burma-Shave's 1936 contest. After being used on roadsigns, it appeared in a booklet published by the Burma-Shave people in 1938. It has been reprinted many times since then—most recently in the *Shepherd Bulletin* dated February 26, 1951." No other information is available as to the final disposition of this problem.

When Mrs. Robert Babcock of Hydesville, California, won the major prize in the 1952 Burma-Shave jingle contest of $1,000.00, she possessed a solid sum of money, perhaps $10,000 in 1990's dollars. Her jingle:

The wife
Who keeps on
Being kissed
Always heads
Her shopping list
Burma-Shave. (497)

"Everybody loved those jingles," Grace Odell said. "They were so humorous and full of fun."

WINNERS
1950 BURMA-SHAVE JINGLE CONTEST

Here are the twenty-four top winners in the Burma-Shave Jingle Contest which closed February 28, 1950:

$100.00 PRIZE WINNERS: Marguerite Beatty, P. O. Box 9639, Pittsburgh, 26, Pa.; Dana Blackmarr, 418 W. Delavan Ave., Buffalo 13, N. Y.; Mrs. James W. Boyd, 110 So. Second St., Austin, Minn.; Douglas Campbell, 238 Watchung Ave., N. Plainfield, N. J.; John D. Dodd, 2825 Arbor St., Ames, Iowa; Louise Ewick, 207 Grove Ave., Dayton, Ohio; Mrs. Frank R. Flower, 8 East Drive, Margate City, N. J.; Robert T. Gidley, 3100 Amherst St., Dallas 5, Texas; Winnifred Heleve, 2415 Harriet Ave. S., Minneapolis 5, Minn.; Walter Jansson, 7400 S. Union Ave., Chicago 21, Ill.

Also, Mrs. Charles Majoros, 6778 Buckingham St., Allen Park, Mich.; Ruth T. Parish, 56 9th St., Lynchburg, Va.; Charles R. Price, 4110 45th St., San Diego 5, Calif.; Ladie Will Ramsey, Fairburn, Ga.; L. P. Roberts, 35 F Street, Salt Lake City, Utah; Mrs. W. N. Sanders, RFD 1, Box 652-B, Bessemer, Ala.; C. W. Schulmeyer, 1758 E. Clinton St., Frankford, Ind.; Reginald W. Stevens, 5036 Irving St., Philadelphia, Pa.; R. E. Wegner, Box 134, Hales Corners, Wisc.; and Amanda Worthington, 255 So. Broadway, Greenville, Miss.

$50.00 PRIZE WINNERS: Pauline Aldrich, R. 1, Box 119, Otis, Ore.; and Clarence M. Lucey, 270 Bridge St., Northampton, Massachusetts.

$25.00 PRIZE WINNERS: Mrs. Miles C. Johnson, 707 No. Armstrong, Litchfield, Minn.; and Lyle E. Thompson, Barnevald, Wisconsin.

BURMA-VITA COMPANY
Minneapolis 5, Minnesota

Chapter 5

MAKING SIGNS

*N*ew jingles required new signs, which required a new division of Burma-Vita, the paint sign shop. George Hamley Odell remembers working in the paint shop during the summers between his school years, with John Kammerer, who ran the shop.

One of George's unforgettable memories was paint day, about once a month, when great dollies filled with boards cut to specifications (10 by 36 inches, initially, but as highway speeds increased, the signs were enlarged to 18 by 40 inches) were wheeled out next to a great vat filled with paint primer. George said two people did the job. Each person grabbed two boards, separated by fingers held between the boards, and dipped the entire boards into the primer. Once coated with primer, two rows of the boards were set on pegs above a slanted metal runner that led down into the vat. The extra paint dripped off the boards, into the runner, and back into the vat. The process was repeated until about a hundred boards, fifty on each aisle beside the vat, would be drip-drying. Once dry, the painted boards were stacked on a storage dolly, and more plain boards were wheeled out. When several dollysful had dried, the same process was repeated in painting the sign backgrounds. During different eras, signs sported orange, blue and red backgrounds, with black or white lettering. The most common were red with white lettering. Blue signs were only used in South Dakota, which had a law preventing red signs used for anything except stop signs. Later, longer-lasting aluminum veneers were dipped into the vats instead of boards.

21

Clinton B. Odell (on the left) worked with Burdette Booth (right) in Burma-Vita's paint shop, stencilling new signs.

Once the primer and paint coats dried, then the boards (or aluminum sheets) were stencilled. George said, "There was a method to it, but it was no secret. You just lined up the boards, and took stencils and put them up against the board or the aluminum, and used a can of white spray paint, and then hung them up to dry." George said the paint shop was often so toxic with fumes that he remembers nearly passing out several times.

Lettering on the signs started at 3¼ inches high, and eventually went to four inches.

Chapter 6

DOCTORS OF DIGGOGRAPHY

Phds to the rescue! More Burma-Shave success meant more signs had to be erected. Those charged with the job were affectionately dubbed Phds, or "post-hole diggers."

Twenty to twenty-five new jingles were added to Burma-Shave's repertoire each year, along with hundreds—even thousands—of new signs, first in the midwest, and eventually in forty-five states.

Evelyn Dorman said that Massachusetts did not have signs either, due to their winding roads. Company president Clinton M. Odell wrote in *Burma-Shavings* in 1945 that signs had been erected in forty-four states. However, signs were erected for another twenty years, and all other later references, as well as grandson Clinton B. Odell, claim forty-five states had signs.

FOR FACES
THAT GO PLACES

ᘒurma ᘒhavings

Allan G. Odell, Editor

ISSUED BY
BURMA VITA CO.
MINNEAPOLIS

NOVEMBER, 1945   VICTORY ISSUE   NUMBER 36

WAR'S END

It has become apparent in the few short weeks since World War No. 2 ended that some good came out of

ROAD SIGN WORK INCREASED AS POSTWAR PROJECT

23

There was a method to the erection of signs. Richard and Joan Dunlop wrote in "What Happened to the Burma-Shave Signs?" in *Home & Away* magazine, that in the early days: "Leonard drove a truckload of fresh signs into virgin territory while Allan ranged ahead in a car until he found a good spot by the road. He looked for straightaways long enough for motorists to have a chance to read each word." Rowsome wrote that the right-of-way needed to be even with the road, to four feet lower, but never higher.

Sharon Carter added in the February 1997 *American History* magazine that advance men went out from the company to scout out suitable locations for the signs. "Prerequisites included the absence of other advertising that would block part of the series from view, a fairly level section of roadway, and good visibility. People were sure to complain if signs were placed in such a way that passers-by missed one of the sequence because of a curve in the road."

Dunlops added, "When Leonard came grinding up with the truck, Allan would already have made the deal." Burma-Shave was generous with their products; they gave products away as incentive to farmers to put the signs on their land initially; they also sent packages of Burma-Vita products to the farmers from time to time; and they paid rent to keep the signs up, up to twenty-five dollars a year, and sent farmers the *Burma-Shavings* newsletter, which gave them the sense that they were part of a larger Burma-Shave family.

Once the rent had been agreed upon (it varied from farmer to farmer), and a few products given away, and permission granted, the brothers broke out spades and dug holes for the sets of six signs. Signs were planted anywhere from 100 paces to 100 feet apart (most likely the latter).

The signs were each meant to be read in two to three seconds at about thirty-five miles per hour. That mere eighteen seconds was far more time than newspaper, magazine, or even other billboard advertisers could hope to get from their readers.

Carter said, "Once the signs had been in place for a while, the advance men would convert themselves into salesmen, visiting the local drugstores, and writing up the orders generated by the new signs." They also learned a hard lesson when they gave out samples at wrestling matches,

Some farmers had to be called out of the field to see if they would give permission for Burma-Shave signs to be set up.

baseball games, and other sporting events; the audience at one wrestling match got incensed with one wrestler and threw hundreds of bottles of Burma-Shave into the ring. Luckily nobody was hurt. After that, the advance men handed out the samples after the event.

Sign diggers spent a lot of time on the road, and worked extremely hard. Clinton B. Odell, son of Allan Odell, said in *The Signs and Rhymes of Burma-Shave* video, "I was just out of college [when I erected signs] and figured I was in pretty good shape, but I had no idea what kind of shape I was in until we went out and dug the holes for those signs. Normally they'd put up five to seven sets a day. Initially I could dig one or two holes, and my partner would do four to five, and at the end of the day I'd be exhausted. It took me two or three weeks until I was in good enough shape to keep up and do my share." Milo Kaiser, who dug thousands of holes for the signs, said it once took him eight hours to dig in a set of signs in Pennsylvania, although it usually only took him an hour per set.

Within four years of installing the first signs, more than 6,000 sets had been set up, and eight trucks with "Burma-Shave" on the side and a smiley face became familiar fare as they crisscrossed the United States, changing rhymes on the signs, at first every year, and then as expenses and sheer numbers of signs mounted, every two years. World War II caused a hiatus of four years between sign changes. Clinton B. Odell said, "A map behind my father's desk (Allan Odell) related each set of signs. Each pin represented a set, so eventually there were 7,000 pins in it. The map was always kept up to date, and he always knew where all the signs were."

Allan G. Odell showed his brother Leonard the locations of all the Burma-Shave signs across the United States. Each pin stuck in the map represented one set of six signs. Before everything was said and done, the map contained 7,000 pins.

Because the trucks made such frequent trips, many people thought Burma-Vita was a larger company than it really was. In actuality, Burma-Vita never employed more than thirty-five people.

George Hamley Odell, youngest son of Allan and Grace Odell, said he worked one summer (about 1960) putting up signs. He spent a month and a half on roads from Minneapolis through the Dakotas to about fifty miles east of Seattle, and then doubled back and went back on Highway 12, through Mobridge. "I remember Mobridge," he laughed, "because I wrecked the truck there, and we had to stay there for a while and have the thing repaired so we could get back to Minneapolis. I was with another guy who was an old hand at working with the signs."

That long trip was mostly spent correcting mistakes a previous sign-installer had made. Burma-Vita had found it more cost-effective to tack up aluminum sheets containing new jingles over the old jingles on the wood signs, instead of the additional work of using special tools to remove the recessed bolts that held the boards, and then screwing on another board.

"You left the first set [of wooden signs] up, but stapled a sort of aluminum facing to the front of the sign," George said. "That aluminum facing had the same red background and white lettering on it as the other signs. You had to be real careful when you stapled on the new sign, and make sure it was on solidly, because many things could undo the stapled-on overlay, like cows rubbing against them, the wind, all sorts of things."

Another hazard was shoddy work. "The last guy who went out there before us hadn't put enough staples in the signs, so they were coming off. But they were coming off selectively, so you would have one or two off per set."

So old signs were showing up in the midst of the new signs, making the jingles nonsensical:

> Said Farmer Brown
> Who's Bald
> To Mars
> For 900
> Rotate the crop
> Burma-Shave.

The missing sign parts brought a double meaning to this Burma-Shave sign from 1958:

> Slow down, pa
> Sakes alive
> Ma missed signs
> Four
> And five
> Burma-Shave. (Verse 25)

Signs disappeared, were knocked down, and the aluminum replacement sheets fell off if not stapled on well.

27

George and his truckdriver took a supply of stencilled replacement sheets of aluminum and checked all signs along several thousand miles of roads. They discovered many signs off, so they replaced them, stapling the replacements on solidly.

George said, "We straightened up signs that were crooked, and we may have put in several new signposts that had gone bad. There was no pattern to the signs that had come down; in fact, we were looking for a pattern, so we could get a better idea of how the last guy had done his work. But he had been a pretty slipshod operator all the way along, so it was just random."

George remembered they had company productivity goals to meet on the trip. "But since I wasn't senior officer, I didn't pay much attention, but the guy who was with me did. I was basically an assistant."

His uncle Leonard once said he had dug every sign hole in the Midwest. "I learned the business from three feet under the ground and up."

Anti-Billboarders Didn't Include Burma-Shave

Anti-billboard sentiment built up from time to time; but surprisingly, Burma-Shave signs came through untouched. Dunlops wrote, "In the 1930s a national furor arose against billboards, which grew so rankly beside American roads. But the discrete little Burma-Shave signs went unscathed. Safety experts, in fact, chimed in with praise, pointing out that motorists slowed down to read them."

However, even Burma-Vita couldn't stay untouched forever. In a front page article in a 1932 *Burma-Shavings*, Burma-Vita reproduced an article by Carl W. Funk (which had been first printed in the *Minneapolis Star* newspaper on January 14, 1932), titled "Outdoor Advertising." In it, Funk chastised women's and other organizations for not thinking through the consequences of outlawing billboards: loss of jobs and revenues most particularly, and is sure that if they had known, they wouldn't have pushed such action.

Eventually, set-back laws (the distance signs had to be from the road) became a problem for the company, particularly in North Carolina, where, in November 1941, the North Carolina Highway Department started removing the Burma-Shave signs, claiming the signs didn't meet new set-back regulations.

Some farmers with signs on their property actually stopped highway department employees from taking down the signs, and reported the problems to Burma-Vita.

It was pure government folderol. The North Carolina Highway Department indeed had issued a regulation that all new signs had to be set back at least fifty feet from the center of roads; additionally, they said all existing signs needn't comply until November 1942.

Unfortunately, the department evidently didn't read its own provision, because on November 1, 1941, a year early, they began removing existing Burma-Shave signs.

Once the mistake was brought to the attention of the highway department, they acknolwedged their mistake, and replaced some of the signs they had taken down. Clinton M. Odell wrote in the *Burma-Shavings* newsletter that Burma-Shave signs would remain in their present locations at least until the next fall.

World War II also caused problems for Burma-Shave signs. A survey of Florida traffic showed that only half of the state's cars were running, a percentage that doubtless held true for the rest of America. That halved the effectiveness of Burma-Shave advertising. Clinton M. Odell noted at least one of the reasons in *Burma-Shavings*: "We, like other users of trucks, have a tire problem. We must conserve our tires; we can't get any more."

In the same 1942 issue, Odell asked lessors to help keep up the signs. He said it took but a minute or two to fix a tipped or turned sign. He also asked people to write Burma-Vita if a sign was missing or when they fixed a sign. Odell said no decrease in sign rental was contemplated. Burma-Vita had enough signs already finished, they figured, to last through 1942.

Most sign materials were needed for the war effort, and simply weren't available: steel for the posts, paint, gasoline, rubber, and more.

Burma-Vita was concerned, but another problem caused more concern: anti-billboard people redoubled their efforts to get rid of signs, with the pro-billboard people's efforts weakened due to war requirements.

When the war ended in 1945, farmers received good news from Burma-Vita: a wholesale fix-up job would take place on the signs all over the country.

Clinton M. Odell wrote in *Burma-Shavings* that "With the war finally over, we are beginning the biggest road sign job for Burma-Shave that has been undertaken since the signs were originally installed. At present we are busily replacing equipment and painting signs. Lumber, posts, paint, trucks, tires . . . are being purchased as fast as possible to put us in position to tackle the big job on the Burma-Shave signs."

More than 2,000 sets of signs were destroyed during wartime years; sign fixing started in the south and headed north. After a year, a thousand sets had been replaced. Clinton M. Odell wrote, "Last summer we used the last of the boards we had on hand to replace some of the red signs in the east and middle west that were badly faded. This work was carried on quite extensively in the northeastern states so the Burma-Shave signs in that territory look pretty good at present.

"Next year new copy on orange boards will replace the present red Burma-Shave signs all over the country. Both you and we can happily look forward to next summer's new dress for the little Burma-Shave signs."

Burma-Shave signs also ran into another problem: many counties had begun to pass local ordinances against signs, which restricted how many Burma-Shave signs could be erected.

And yet, nothing in those first twenty years stopped or even slowed down Burma-Shave. At its peak, Burma-Shave had 40,000 signs on properties all over the United States, one of the greatest advertising strategies and success stories of all time.

After the company was sold to Phillip Morris Company in 1963, new and larger signs were tried, so the speeding public would have more opportunity to read the signs; but Philip Morris discovered what the Odells had already known: the cost was prohibitive.

Grace Odell said, "The signs couldn't work today, because they would have to be put back so far from the road that you couldn't see them. Burma-Shave signs in those days was perhaps like Shangri-la," Grace said wistfully.

CHEER UP FACE
THE WAR IS OVER

𝕭urma-𝕾havings

Allan G Odell-Editor

ISSUED BY THE
BURMA-VITA CO.
MINNEAPOLIS

JUNE 1930   JOBBERS ISSUE   NUMBER 1

Chapter 7

FRIEND FARMER AND
BURMA-SHAVINGS NEWSLETTER

*I*n one of the earliest issues of *Burma-Shavings*, Burma-Vita's newsletter to farmers and business people, editor Allan G. Odell wrote: "Martin O. Hildebrand wrote us from Huntington, Indiana, in December expressing appreciation for our paper and continued as follows, 'My little ten-year-old grandson, Jack, of South Bend, said, "Hello, grandpa, I see you are up to date with your Burma-Shave sign boards." I assure you I will

Farmers were the best friends that Burma-Shave had.

see them kept in shape as I count them as a real asset to my beautiful suburban home.' Hurrah for Jack Hildebrand and his granddad!"

Those were the kinds of letters that Burma-Vita received from the people on whom the company most depended: America's farmers.

Burma-Shave would never have happened without the farmers. "They were just absolutely marvelous," said Grace Odell, Allan's wife.

Farmers were even highlighted in the jingles:

> Said farmer Brown
> Who's bald
> On Top
> "Wish I could
> Rotate the crop."
> Burma-Shave. (Verse 26)

and developed incredible loyalty to Burma-Shave.

Farmers not only bought Burma-Vita products, but, most important, they allowed Burma-Shave signs to be placed on their land. Burma-Shave probably wouldn't have worked without them.

In compensation, farmers received occasional packages of free products from Burma-Vita, a small rental payment for keeping the signs on the farms, and the *Burma-Shavings* newsletter.

The *Burma-Shavings* newsletter allowed farmers to feel like one of the Burma-Shave family members. In it Burma-Vita published an honor roll of farmers who maintained their own signs, or lost parts of them or had them stolen, and then wrote in for new ones (Burma-Vita would even send out the special wrench they needed to put the signs up properly).

One of the widely-read parts of *Burma-Shavings* was its "Honorable Mention" (later "Honor Roll"): ". . . a carefully prepared list of our lessors who since the previous issue have advised us that, through some specified action, they have helped us maintain our signs. It may have consisted in only trimming down some weeds that partially interfered with the view of the signs, it may have been that one or more boards have been replaced by the property owner; in some cases it may have been complete installation of a whole set. We appreciate that much work is done for us that we never hear about, for this we are truly grateful, but would like, if possible, to publicly acknowledge any service, however small."

FRIENDS

Again we greet you good friends with a few choice excerpts from your many friendly letters.

Mr. P. R. Malone of Waco, Texas, writes that he had just made a special trip out to check the Burma-Shave signs.

Thank you, Mr. Malone. We know we can depend on you to keep our signs in good shape.

From Grand Rapids, Ohio, comes a friendly card from August Schultz who informs us that he, his two sons and his son-in-law all use Burma-Shave and recommend it highly.

Mr. Schultz, it is not only a privilege to have you as one of our lessors but we want you to know that we greatly appreciate having you and your family as valued customers.

Jack Smith of Keystone, Ala., tells us that he has repaired signs broken by Hallowe'en pranksters.

It is little extra services like this, Mr. Smith, that really show us how many splendid friends we really have.

F. H. Abbott of Burlington, Vt., writes this short statement that means so much — "Signs have been replaced."

You don't realize, Mr. Abbott, what your statement means to us. It is the real proof that our friends are with us when we need them most. Thank you so much.

A kind letter offering help from Mrs. T. E. Lillard of Norwalk, Calif., wishes us Merry Christmas and Happy New Year.

Thank you, Mrs. Lillard; we sincerely wish we knew each of our friends better. Your kind wishes were gratefully accepted.

Many letters from North Carolina like that from Mr. W. P. Edwards of Neuse, N. C., arrived during the late Fall informing us of removal of our signs by the Highway Department.

We are grateful to you, Mr. Edwards, and the other fine N. C. people who wrote us so promptly. It was your quick action which enabled us to get the Highway Department to right the wrong it had committed. The Highway Department was very fine in admitting their mistake and did everything possible to restore our signs.

Mr. L. W. Holland of Cape May, N. J., writes us about a missing sign and offers help in repairing it.

Thank you, Mr. Holland, we greatly appreciate your thoughtfulness and offer of help.

A letter from Mrs. Elsie Bauer of Longmont, Colo., states that she had our signs repaired the same day the material arrived.

Your promptness is much appreciated, Mrs. Bauer. You and Mr. Bauer are truly friends to be proud of.

C. C. Ergle of Winston, Ga., writes, "I have replaced signs and they are in good shape."

Such reassuring information is good to get, Mr. Ergle. Thank you.

Mr. F. A. Swenson of Motley, Minn., repaired our signs and added that the Burma-Shave signs were the best safety signal to motorists that he had ever seen.

Thank you, Mr. Swenson, we are constantly endeavoring to do our bit toward highway safety and it is a pleasure to receive your letter and thousands of others each year commending us for our highway safety campaign.

Last but not least we have a letter from Homer P. Whitlow of Rocky Mount, Va., who very kindly states he was glad to be of service to us.

You know, Mr. Whitlow, your friendliness depicts exceptionally well the spirit behind all of these fine letters. We want you all to know that we are grateful for your attitude toward us and we will always endeavor to warrant your good will.

Thank you, good friends; space is the only factor which prohibits our printing all of your kind and helpful letters.

When you've done your best you feel pretty good, even though you haven't made much money.

HONOR ROLL

The following men and women have written us since the last issue of "BURMA-SHAVINGS" that they have extended help in the maintenance of our signs.

ALABAMA
Jack Smith................Keystone
Mrs. J. E. Gachet..........Prattville

ARKANSAS
A. C. Raper................Little Rock
Mrs. L. A. Strozyk....N. Little Rock

CALIFORNIA
Mrs. Con Nevin.............Hayward
Mrs. T. E. Lillard..........Norwalk
Agnes J. Rae............San Francisco
A. C. Hanks...............Dunnigan
O. Rosenbaum....San Juan Capistrano
Lmelia Skinner............Victorville
Sam Basile.................Sonoma
Carl Pizzi.................Granada
Hans Struve...............Watsonville
Carl Buck..................Gilroy
Peter Nosero..............Fontana

COLORADO
Mrs. Elsie Bauer...........Longmont

GEORGIA
C. C. Ergle...............Winston
W. M. Brock..............Resaca
R. E. Cotten...........Milledgeville
S. E. Denman.............Ringgold

ILLINOIS
William F. Knauer.........Elizabeth

INDIANA
Stephen J. Campbell.......LaFayette
Melissa Harper..........New Haven

KANSAS
Mrs. John Wohlford........Murdock
E. J. Chesky..............Herington
R. B. Riordan.............Solomon
Merl Howe.................Wichita
C. T. Reichr..............Inman
W. L. Richards............Lecompton

KENTUCKY
J. C. Warren..............Henderson
Mrs. W. H. Bicknell........Berea
Charlie Ruber.............Butler

MAINE
Annie Gilman.........South Portland

MICHIGAN
W. R. Norton.............Plainwell

MINNESOTA
Lester Calkins..........Sauk Centre
F. A. Swenson.............Motley

MISSOURI
Mrs. I. N. Holland........Savannah

NEBRASKA
Delmer Helmke.............Pickrell
S. F. Heim................Dawson

NEW HAMPSHIRE
R. L. Williams............Dover
Mrs. Mary B. Aldrich......Mascoma

NEW JERSEY
L. W. Holland............Cape May

NEW YORK
William Van Auken.....Duanesburg
F. C. Martin..............Bullville

NORTH CAROLINA
Gus Murchison.............Gulf
W. P. Edwards.............Neuse
Mrs. M. L. Poole..........Cameron
J. T. Hiatt...............Lexington
J. L. DeGraff.......Guilford College
O. L. Pegram.............Stokesdale
E. F. Walker.............High Point

NORTH DAKOTA
James W. Dolyniuk.........Belfield
George Newport............Minot

OHIO
O. J. Post............Chagrin Falls
August Schultz.......Grand Rapids

OKLAHOMA
D. E. Shaffer.............Marietta
A. J. Nichols.............Marietta
J. Thomas.................Davis

OREGON
Gottfried Fossbind........Tillamook
Chas. R. Moore............Tillamook

PENNSYLVANIA
R. P. Buhan...............Stoyestown
A. L. Hauer...............Lebanon
J. Milton Benner..........Gettysburg
Daniel A. Sell...........Littlestown

TEXAS
P. R. Malone..............Waco
W. C. Moore...............Sanger
A. D. Speer...............Harwood
W. P. Reeves..............Houston
W. F. Thompson............Decatur
J. U. King..............Fort Worth
E. R. Qualls..............Hillsboro
R. E. Ellis............Fort Worth
Mrs. A. J. Lowrey.........Wilmer
Jerome Wylie..............Rhome
Wm. Helweg...............Encinal
Joe Bullinger............Henrietta
Wm. Goodlow..............Skidmore
G. W. Heard.............Hempstead
S. E. Carroll............Texarkana
Claude Capps..............Elgin

UTAH
H. T. Williams..........Springville
Pearl Johnson.......Salt Lake City

VERMONT
F. H. Abbott.............Burlington

VIRGINIA
Homer P. Whitlow......Rocky Mount
Fannie Bailey............Wakefield
Mrs. B. W. Cummings..Prince George
E. E. Carlton......South Richmond
Mrs. W. A. Drinkard..Concord Depot
W. D. Young...........Sydnorsville
W. H. Smithers............Ashland
L. B. Amory...............Grafton
Jno. B. Grimes...........Smithfield
Irvin L. Rakes...........Elliston
Mrs. Ettie Brown.........Hematite
Rev. Watt J. Bailey......Waverly
T. Ashby Smith...........Sterling
Cabell King............Gordonsville
W. W. Butler..............Bumpass
Mrs. George E. Sims......Richmond

WASHINGTON
Wm. Sanders...............Bothell
Alex Graham...............Olympia

WISCONSIN
Arthur Duesing.........Green Bay
Wm. Belitz...............Manitowoc

A 1942 letter shows the friendliness of Burma-Vita: "F.H. Abbott of Burlington, Vt., writes this short statement that means so much—'Signs have been replaced.' You don't realize, Mr. Abbott, what your statement means to us. It is the real proof that our friends are with us when we need them most. Thank you so much."

Burma-Shavings often published letters from these same lessors:

"Edward Skalitzky of Waterloo, Wis., writes: Three Burma-Shave signs on my farm were destroyed, and one post broken off. Please send me new signs and I will replace them. Would you also please keep me informed at all times about the roadside zoning bill? I will do all I can to defeat this bill.

"Thank you, Mr. Skalitzky. Your help in maintaining our signs is appreciated. We are also grateful for the interest shown in the Wisconsin zoning laws.

"Audie Michael and Dilla Brook, Rivesville, W. Va., advise us: Your sign on our property is O.K.—in perfect condition.

"Our thanks to you, Audie Michael and Dilla Brook—we are always glad to get this kind of information."

"Fred Christensen, Elma, Wash., Ernest DeVine, Ferrisburg, Vt., and J.U. Ross, Tangent, Ore., reported damage by Halloween pranksters.

"Thank you, folks, for this information. These signs will be repaired at an early date.

"From Mrs. William Holm of Van Horne, Iowa: We fixed your sign post, and the sign board. The post was broken off, and the board was split through twice. It is good as new again now.

"We greatly appreciate receiving this information from Mrs. Holm.

"From W.K. Butler, Bumpass, Va.: Your signs on my property are in good condition. I look after them and see that they stay in good shape. There are no other signs on my property.

"Thank you, Mr. Butler, for your 100% cooperation."

"Mrs. Blocher, Burton, Ore., writes as follows: Someone has taken two of your signs away. I cannot find them. Four were down, but I put two of them back. Stakes and all were taken. Advise.

"Thank you very much, Mrs. Blocher, for this information.

"A.W. Adriaenssens, of Stroud, Okla., sends this information: I will do all I can to help defeat the roadsign bills. I try to take good care of your signs. Two or three months ago I found one sign down, and the post split almost down. I drove home for tools and nails, and it is as good as ever now.

"Mr. Adriaenssens, thank you. This sort of cooperation is deeply appreciated."

Along with the solid information and opinions, *Burma-Shavings* also published humorous stories: "We had a report from the crew in South Dakota a short time ago explaining a delay in their schedule due to motor trouble and it read something like the following: Stuck in the northern Black Hills with two spark plugs shot—walked to a farmhouse and asked for a spare plug—was told by farmhand that he didn't chew but he could let us have some 'snoose.'"

Each issue of *Burma-Shavings* also contained various jokes:

"Mr. Brown handed his wife a roll of bills. 'Now that we've struck oil, Mary, I want you to buy yourself some decent clothes.'

"'Bill Brown, I want you to know I've always worn decent clothes. From now on, I'm going to dress like other women.'

"Mother was lecturing her small son about his conduct. 'Never do anything you would be ashamed to have the whole world watch you do.'

"'Whoopee!' whooped the boy. 'No more baths for me. I sure wouldn't want the whole world to watch me take a bath.'"

Also, these pithy sayings:

"'You can save yourself lots of trouble by not borrowing it.'

'Don't question your wife's judgment—look whom she married.'

'When money talks, nobody pays much attention to the grammar.'

'When Noah sailed the ocean blue
He had his troubles same as you.
For days and nights he drove his ark
Before he found a place to park.'"

Despite the smallness of the recompense farmers received for having the signs on their land, the money was important to them, and no more so than during the Depression. Many farmers were greatly relieved to find out through the *Burma-Shavings* that rentals would remain the same in 1932. Sign-rent renewals were handled through self-addressed, stamped envelopes sent out by Burma-Vita.

Clinton M. Odell often closed his "President's Corner" column in unusual ways. In the 1932 one he ended: "Now all together!

> Half a pound
> For
> Half a dollar
> At the drug store
> Simply holler
> Burma-Shave. (Verse 27)

Cordially yours,
CLINTON M. ODELL"

Burma-Shavings took a solid stance on issues that affected the company, as when Allan wrote in very pointed language: "Another comment comes from Belvedere, South Dakota. Edith Grayner says, 'I am glad to be one of the lucky farmers that has a Burma-Shave set of signs on my farm for when I receive my check I always say it is the only check I ever received off my place that I did not have to work for.'

"By the way, Miss Grayner, do you realize that some of our bright legislators, who are always looking for more money to spend, are trying to prevent your receiving such checks? Although you already pay real estate taxes on your land and should be able to use this land for your own special benefit as you see fit . . . these agitators want to tax outdoor signs to such an extent that the advertisers can't afford to keep them up and out the signs go.

"Your state is O.K. We like South Dakota. As a matter of fact we don't mind a reasonable tax, but in some states, Maryland for instance, we are taxed six times for each set just because we use six little separate boards in a group. Needless to say, there are a lot of Maryland farmers who would like to have our signs on their places, but we can't afford them and the Maryland farmer loses out."

The newsletter also informed people about Burma-Shave prices, and the numbers of people using the product. It also showed the locations of the signs, from time to time, using a large United States map stuck full of pins.

In 1930, six trucks were zipping around the country changing the copy on Burma-Shave signs and digging in new ones where appropriate. The first jingle contest had been held, and one of the winners has been one of the most-beloved of all Burma-Shave rhymes:

> Does your husband
> Misbehave
> Grunt and grumble
> Rant and rave
> Shoot the brute some
> Burma-Shave. (Verse 28)

Burma-Shavings was the company information bulletin, cheerleader, and cementer of good relations with farmers, because the Odells clearly knew that without the farmer, Burma-Vita probably would not have survived.

FOR FACES THAT GO PLACES

Burma Shavings

ISSUED BY BURMA VITA CO. MINNEAPOLIS

MARCH, 1950

NUMBER 45

Burma-Shave Covers The Nation

MORE BURMA-SHAVE SIGNS . . . WEST COAST, ALABAMA COMPLETED

Extensive work on the west coast was carried on last fall, and later started in Alabama. This re-vamping job was caused by the fact that many locations had deteriorated, or had been taken out during the war, and also by the fact that lessors had allowed other signs to go in between the Burma-Shave signs.

We sent a crew of three men out to cover Washington and Oregon, and it took about three months to complete the job. Our inferior locations were cancelled, and many new locations were bought.

Work in Alabama was carried on in January and February, 1950. Alabama hadn't been gone over carefully since 1932 when the locations were first purchased. During that period of time we had lost about half of our locations in the state for various reasons—knocked down, cancelled during the war, etc., and we didn't have enough signs in the state to be of much value to us. Our crew reported excellent locations now in Alabama, and we are looking forward to a long and friendly relationship with all of our new lessors, as well as the old ones, in this state. We feel that the residents of Alabama are going to protect the Burma-Shave signs, and are not going to allow the locations to be ruined by permitting other signs to be placed in the set.

PRESIDENT'S CORNER

It gives me a great deal of pleasure to state that during the past few years when we have been re-vamping the Burma-Shave sign locations, we have found that our lessors on the whole have proved exceedingly loyal. I drove east last fall, and covered parts of Wisconsin, Illinois, Indiana, Ohio, etc., and was delighted to see locations that had been put up 20 years ago still in as good condition as they were the day the leases were originally made. Most of our lessors in these states seem to have taken a genuine interest in the Burma-Shave signs, because on the whole, I found the locations without obstructions, and the signs standing in good shape.

This gave me one of the biggest thrills of my life, because it showed that the policy of fairness which Burma-Vita Company has always shown its lessors, was paying dividends. Thank you very much for your kind cooperation.

Allen G. Odell,
President.

Large Sign Expansion Program Now Under Way Throughout United States

Did you know that the Burma-Shave signs on your property are an integral part of an advertising plan that is a national institution? Our signs cover the nation coast to coast, and from Canada to the Gulf, and appear in forty-four states.

When war struck we had approximately 7,000 sets of signs. During the years of the war when manpower, trucks, lumber, etc., were not available, we lost approximately 2,000 sets of signs. Since the close of the war we have been building the signs up as fast as we could, until we now have about 6,000 sets of signs, in good condition, and hope to go beyond the 7,000 mark soon.

These signs, of necessity, have created a business employing a good many people. Lumber is bought in carload lots, and we keep a crew of men busy painting, and lettering the signboards. They are later assembled, and installed by crews, travelling in large trucks out of Minneapolis.

It costs the company a large amount of money each year to paint, place, maintain the signs, and pay rental on same. Our road crews, when they are not installing signs, are checking existing signs, straightening them, making minor repairs, etc., so our signs will at all times be in ship-shape order. In this connection we very much appreciate any help our lessors give us in maintaining the signs, when we do not have crews working in their vicinity. (See Honorable Mention, next page.)

The expansion program of the Burma-Shave signs is not being pushed in states that have drastic roadsign laws on the books. We hope our lessors will do all they can to prevent this sort of legislation, so that they will not be deprived of any rights they now have. Many states have passed "County Enabling Acts," which permit each county, if it so desires, to pass local ordinances directed against signs. The difficulty we have had in fighting county zoning ordinances, is that we don't hear about them, and

(Continued on Back Page)

Chapter 8

FREE! FREE! A TRIP TO MARS!

I n 1958 Arlyss "Frenchy" French, the manager of a Red Owl grocery store in Appleton, Wisconsin, saw a new set of Burma-Shave signs on a road between Fond du Lac and Sheboygan, Wisconsin:

> Free—free
> A trip
> To Mars
> For 900
> Empty Jars
> Burma-Shave. (Verse 29)

"I saw the ad on the road," Frenchy said, "and I kept wondering, 'What the Sam Hill would they do if someone came up with 900 empty jars?'

Although his Red Owl store carried Burma-Shave, the product had never been a big seller, he said. "We'd always sold Burma-Shave, but not a lot of it. I had a big grocery store, and maybe that's why.

"That set of signs worked on me so hard that I ordered 900 full jars, and made a display in the middle of the store. I trimmed that store all up: 'Buy Burma-Shave, send Frenchy to Mars,' and all that."

When customers bought a jar of Burma-Shave, Frenchy scraped out the jar and poured the shaving cream into an empty ice-cream container so he could keep the jar. "In about three months we had the 900 empty jars."

Frenchy sent Burma-Vita a telegram asking where he should ship the 900 empty jars. Allan sent Frenchy this jingle back:

> If a trip
> To Mars
> You'd earn
> Remember friend
> There's no return.
> Burma-Shave.

Now it was Frenchy's turn to pen his own jingle:

> Let's not quibble
> Let's not fret
> Gather your forces
> I'm all set.

And the follow-up from Burma-Vita:

> Our rockets are ready
> We ain't splitting hairs
> Just send us the jars—
> And arrange your affairs.

Burma-Vita may originally have been kidding, but Frenchy and his Red Owl supervisor, Jack Wotrang, were dead serious. "Jack was really gung-ho on it, too," Frenchy said. "It sounded like Burma-Shave didn't think anything was going to happen. Other people said they didn't. Finally they sent a man from Minneapolis to see me."

After Ralph Getchman talked with Frenchy, Ralph raced to a telephone and told his bosses at Burma-Vita that Frenchy indeed meant business. By this time, Frenchy was taking out full-page ads in the newspaper and his store was booming, so he wasn't about to slack off. He also built a large model rocket plane for the display, and had little green men on top of the store throwing toy rocket gliders out to people in the store parking lot.

Once Frenchy reached his goal of 900 jars, he made a series of Burma-Shave-like signs, and set them up at intervals in front of his store:

> Have 900
> Jars
> Good-bye
> America
> Hello Mars.

39

Arlyss "Frenchy" French was the manager of a Red Owl supermarket in Appleton, Wisconsin, in 1958 when he wondered what would happen if someone took the Burma-Vita company up on their offer of a free trip to Mars for 900 jars. Here he is shown with a Brinks armored truck filled with the 900 empty Burma-Shave jars he needed.

Frenchy offered one of the 900 empty jars to a smiling Allan Odell (right), president of Burma-Vita Company. Allan would probably be smiling broader if he knew the amount of free advertising Frenchy's ploy would create for Burma-Shave.

Finally Burma-Vita officials acquiesced. Frenchy brought the jars in, and in exchange got a ticket. "I had no idea where I was going until after they'd given me the ticket."

He *was* going to Mars—Moers (pronounced "Mars"), Germany.

About that time the Burma-Shave divisional manager in Green Bay heard about Frenchy and his trip, and he promptly reported to Burma-Vita that Frenchy was a family man and never went anywhere without his wife, so the company should send her, too. "I sometimes think he spent some of his own money to help get Frances to go along to Germany," Frenchy said.

While the Frenches were waiting for the date to report to Minneapolis, Jack convinced Frenchy to construct a space suit. Those who knew Frenchy knew it didn't take much convincing to get it done. "It wasn't much of a space suit, I'll tell you," Frenchy said. "There hadn't been anybody in space yet, so we made a flight suit just as an attention getter."

Frenchy and Allan Odell in front of the Red Owl grocery store before Frenchy was sent to Mars (actually Moers—pronounced "Mars"—Germany).

In mid-December 1958, Frenchy showed up in Minneapolis wearing a bubble suit on his head, a silver space suit with a large Red Owl logo on his chest and made his grand entrance. He was whisked away to the home of the president of Burma-Shave, Allan Odell. Additionally, Red Owl had rented a Brink's armored truck to deliver the jars, and the truck was covered with signs expounding Frenchy's new-found status, saying that Frenchy should be sent to Mars.

By this time, Frenchy found himself wondering what was going on. "You know what I mean. I was thinking, 'What's going to be next?' It was pretty fast for a country boy like I am."

He and Frances were flown to New York, where they met with the area Burma-Shave representative. "He really wined and dined us, and took us to a New York stage play. I don't know if I'd ever been to New York or not, but I hadn't seen any of the stage plays, that's for sure. With seven kids, we did take the occasional vacation, but it wasn't that kind." They were also given spending money from Burma-Shave for their European jaunt.

The next morning, Frenchy and Frances boarded a jet airplane to Germany. "Jet flights had just started, so we were on one of the earliest ones."

Because of weather, they couldn't land at Düsseldorf, but were diverted to Paris instead. "The next morning we were supposed to get up early to catch a flight to Düsseldorf, and I asked if it would be all right if we spent a day in Paris, and go to Düsseldorf in the evening. I figured we'd never get to Paris again in our lifetime."

Officials kindly agreed. Burma-Shave hired an English-speaking cab driver, and Frenchy and Frances were shown around Paris.

That evening, they flew to Düsseldorf. "As we were landing, I saw all these people out on the runway and all those cameras, and I said to my wife, 'Boy, there must be somebody important on this plane.'"

At this time, Frenchy's brother-in-law and his wife, Frenchy's sister, were stationed in Germany where the brother-in-law was in the service, just a few miles from Düsseldorf. Nobody was sure what time Frenchy and Frances were coming in from Paris; all the newsmen were asking Frenchy's sister, "Are you sure you'll know him when he comes off the plane?"

Frenchy said, "They watched every plane that came in all day, and finally we walked out of our plane, and she said 'That's him!'"

He walked out of the plane, and all the newspeople were yelling, "Put on your helmet, put on your helmet!" so he did. He was also wearing a hood, which he donned as well. "The cameras were really snapping. We went through customs, and that was the beginning of the fun over there."

The Frenches were assigned an English-speaking woman from the German consulate, and they all drove in a caravan of ten cars to Moers. "Moers is just a crossroads of four houses, one on each corner. But there was a big delegation there to meet us." There he was, on or in, "Mars."

Officials gave Frances a beautiful bouquet of flowers and presented Frenchy with—a bouquet of weeds. "That was something," he laughs. "They also gave me a live little white pig, which is an omen for good luck."

What surprised him most was a Coca-Cola truck and driver that came roaring up. "It stopped right where we were, and the driver came running over with a six-pack of Coke, and put it in my hands, and backed up and took a picture. Then he came right over and took the Coke right out of my hands and went and put it back in the truck. I thought that was something else."

There was a lot of publicity, not only because of the Burma-Shave stunt, but because Frenchy was the first American in the area since Eisenhower had crossed the Rhine at the end of World War II.

They were brought to the parliament at Düsseldorf, and introduced to the politicians.

Next, "They took us to an opera, and we went to the Burgermeister's home and had a big hoopdedoo there. They really took care of us, I'll tell you."

But too soon, the vacation of a lifetime was over. It was time to return. And once Frenchy got back to the United States, everything suddenly changed. He was no celebrity any more. He had had his fifteen minutes of fame.

"They were opening a new Red Owl store in Milwaukee, and they wanted me there for the grand opening. I was there in my suit and so on, but nobody was very interested.

"But I still think the whole thing was a pretty good deal and a pretty good time."

Chapter 9

AMERICA'S FIRST PUBLIC SERVICE
ANNOUNCEMENTS

Burma-Vita was an admirable company, for many reasons—many modern American companies could learn from them. From its formation the company showed inventiveness and creativity in its advertisings with money give-aways, its policy of rejecting questionable rhymes for the signs, the humor and poke-fun-at-ourselves attitude of some of the jingles, the courting of the farmers, give-aways of Burma-Vita products, and much more.

More than that, Burma-Vita pioneered public service jingles. Allan wrote the first one, which appeared in 1935:

> Keep well
> To the right
> Of the oncoming car.
> Get your close shaves
> From the half-pound jar
> Burma-Shave. (Verse 30)

Evelyn Dorman wrote, "In addition to protecting the highways from immoral advertising, the Odells felt they needed to be helpful in terms of not contributing to highway accidents with distracting signs. They tried to instill some sort of goodwill even though billboard backlash in the 1960s would spell the signs'—and the company's—demise." (Although outdoor advertising expert Joe Blackstock, director of research for Eller Media of Los

44

Angeles, and a five-decade veteran of outdoor advertising, didn't think the 1960's billboard backlash made any difference. He said, "There has been a small but vociferous anti-billboard sentiment in all the decades of this century, starting in 1900. It's relatively small, and most people when interviewed or surveyed show that the 1930s for example were no different than the 1920s, and so on. People loved the little Burma-Shave signs. I don't think anybody particularly disliked them. Burma-Shave certainly didn't do the outdoor advertising medium any harm, that's for sure.")

Many signs over the years targeted poor driving, like this 1937 sign:

> Drive
> With care.
> Be alive
> When
> You arrive.
> Burma-Shave. (Verse 31)

A few years later, it seems that Burma-Shave made sure that their safety rhymes included more humor:

> At intersections
> Look each way.
> A harp sounds nice
> But it's
> Hard to play
> Burma-Shave. (Verse 32)

And—

> Trains don't wander
> All over the map
> For no one
> Sits on
> The engineer's lap
> Burma-Shave. (Verse 33)

both from 1941.

1941 also produced this witty one:

> From
> Bar
> To car
> To
> Gates Ajar.
> Burma-Shave. (Verse 34)

In 1942 came this gem:

> Brother speeders
> Let's
> Rehearse
> All together
> "Good morning, nurse!"
> Burma-Shave. (Verse 35)

Also,

> Approached
> A crossing
> Without looking
> Who will eat
> His widow's cooking?
> Burma-Shave. (Verse 36)

Along with another one from 1942,

> If hugging
> On highways
> Is your sport
> Trade in your car
> For a davenport.
> Burma-Shave. (Verse 37)

A girl
Should hold on
To her youth
But not when
He's driving
Burma-Shave. (Verse 38)

was another of the public-service messages from 1942. In 1945:

Big mistake
Many make
Rely on horn
Instead
of brake
Burma-Shave. (Verse 39)

1947:

Don't lose
Your head
To gain a minute
You need your head
Your brains are in it
Burma-Shave. (Verse 40)

And 1949's

He saw
The train
And tried to duck it
Kicked first the gas
And then the bucket
Burma-Shave. (Verse 41)

Some of the Burma-Shave safety signs were very thoughtful:

The minute
Some folks
Save through speed
They never even
Live to need
Burma-Shave. (Verse 42)

As the automobile became more popular, and more Americans drove, the six signs by the side of the road sold more and more Burma-Shave.

Burma-Vita hit on the theme of not drinking while driving as in this 1945 sign:

> If these
> Signs blur
> And bounce around
> You'd better park
> And walk to town
> Burma-Shave. (Verse 43)

48

And this one from 1948:

> The midnight ride
> Of Paul
> For beer
> Led to a
> Warmer hemisphere
> Burma-Shave. (Verse 44)

And

> When frisky
> With whiskey
> Don't drive
> 'cause it's
> Risky
> Burma-Shave. (Verse 45)

Burma-Vita encouraged their contest jinglers to submit public-service rhymes. Part of Burma-Shave's success was this public-service effort; they were light years ahead of their time.

Chapter 10

SIGNS THAT MISFIRED AND BACKFIRED

*E*nglish novelist George Eliot wrote that "A difference of taste in jokes is a great strain on the affections." Thus it was not surprising when some people interpreted some signs in ways the Odells had not intended.

The first time this happened, according to Grace Odell in the Delaney Communications, Inc., video *The Signs and Rhymes of Burma-Shave,* was when the first set of "Free—Free, a trip to Mars, for 900 empty jars," set of signs was set out in 1936. Grace said that, to everyone's amazement, someone called Burma-Vita and said that he had 800 empty jars, and wanted to know what he would get if he brought them in, and where was he supposed to deliver the jars? She said Allan came home very distraught, wondering what to do. She told him to sleep on it, and he would think of something. She reminded him that he always did.

The next day he came up with a return rhyme: "If a trip to Mars you earn, remember friend, there's no return. Burma-Shave." They sent that note back to the man, and Grace said they never heard from him again, and the near disaster was averted.

Until twenty years later. That's when Arlyss French came on the scene with his 900 jars. However, the company actually emerged in a better position because they decided to play along with him instead of fighting him. Because they sent him to Mars (Moers, Germany), the company gathered free international advertising—Frenchy said his trip was written up in newspapers all over Europe as well as the United States—and Burma-Vita also gained valuable good will among its present and future customers.

Other sets of signs caused them trouble, as well. Like this 1933 rhyme that said:

Free offer! Free offer!
Rip a fender
Off your car
Mail it in for
A half-pound jar
Burma-Shave. (Verse 46)

Perhaps Burma-Vita didn't figure anyone would bite on the ditty, but the Great Depression had set in, times were tough, and the offer was for a useful free product. The sign proved to be a mistake; any staple that could be had free would be a boon to a family's economy.

At first shavers sent fenders from toy cars, and, while chuckling, Burma-Vita officials cheerfully sent out their full half-pound jars in return.

Then some people even scoured junkyards for real fenders, which they sent into the Minneapolis offices, until at least twenty-five crates of real fenders had wended their way to Burma-Vita. In great good humor, the Odells mailed out the half-pound jars to all senders. But, not being in the used-car business, they promptly removed the signs.

Another sign got them in trouble in 1948:

The midnight ride
Of Paul
For beer
Led to a
Warmer hemisphere
Burma-Shave. (Verse 44)

This was an innocent one that the Odells figured would work for their driving-not-drinking awareness concept. But, after it came out, beer distributors felt it singled them out. They protested, and the Odells decided to take down the signs.

Incidents like these showed that the company was responsive to public feelings and enhanced its reputation as a company that tried to do the right things.

The humor backfired on Burma-Shave in another and more costly way, as with this 1959 sign :

> This cooling shave
> Will never fail
> To stamp
> Its user
> First-class male.
> Burma-Shave. (Verse 47)

This set as usual contained six signs. Until the second-last sign began to disappear, and, as the Odells noticed, this happened most often around college towns. They figured college-dorm rooms must be plastered with the signs.

The loss of the signs was not only expensive, but it ruined sets all over the United States. To make the removal of the signs more difficult,

Not everyone loved the Burma-Shave signs; some women protested at how they thought the signs portrayed them.

Burma-Vita altered their method for bolting the signs to the posts, indenting the nut into the sign so a special tool was needed to remove it. That at least slowed the thefts down.

One other problem that came about was a charge that Burma-Shave couldn't use at least one of their jingles. Evelyn S. Dorman wrote in the *Encyclopedia of Consumer Brands*: "Barbasol even legally challenged the Burma-Shave jingle "No brush, no lather, no rub-in," alleging that it was Barbasol's exclusive property. A similar line was sung on the radio as the theme song of Barbasol: "Barbasol, Barbasol, no brush, no lather, no rub-in—wet your razor and begin." It is unclear what happened with this allegation.

Though just about everybody liked Burma-Shave signs, there are always those contrary people who didn't. One woman said she never liked the signs. "I always hated them. Charlie looked a lot better in a beard . . . and it seems like every time he saw one of those new Burma-Shave sets of signs he'd shave for a while, and that was worse than ever because then there were all those little prickles that hurt. And so many of those jingles treated women not the way I wanted to be treated, calling us 'tomatoes,' and 'chicks,' and the like. I never did go for that."

Humor is always a two-edged sword, so it is extremely surprising, and a tribute to Burma-Vita's sensitivity and insight into what might bother people that there were not more of the signs that backfired on them.

Chapter 11

THEY WOULDN'T DO THIS TODAY

*T*imes change. With those changed times come different views on race, religion, child care, almost everything. Life during the years when Burma-Shave signs were in their heyday, the 1930s through the 1950s, was a very different time than today. And because life is so different—especially relations between the races and the sexes—a number of Burma-Shave signs would never be used today. One was put up in 1930:

> Uncle Rube
> Buys tube
> One week
> Looks sleek
> Like Sheik.
> Burma-Shave. (Verse 48)

It would doubtless not be used nowadays because of the negative Arab connotations. Also this 1937 one:

> Every
> Sheba
> Wants a Sheik
> Strong of muscle
> Smooth of cheek
> Burma-Shave. (Verse 49)

would probably not have been used for the same reason.

Each Burma-Shave jingle was a little story in itself and reflected a part of Americana. This was one of the ads used in the streetcar card series, when Burma-Shave abandoned signs by the side of the road for a while. The sentiment today probably would not be politically correct.

Women and women's organizations and others likely wouldn't have liked this 1936 set:

> If you
> And whiskers
> Do hobnob
> Some sailor gob
> Will steal your squab.
> Burma-Shave. (Verse 50)

Or from 1945:

> Why does a chicken
> Cross the street?
> Shes sees a guy
> She'd like to meet.
> He uses
> Burma-Shave. (Verse 51)

And

> The chick
> He wed
> Let out a whoop
> Felt his chin and
> Flew the coop
> Burma-Shave. (Verse 52)

from 1945 (when a huge number of Americans married after World War II ended). Then from 1950:

> His cheek
> Was rough
> His chick vamoosed
> And now she won't
> Come home to roost.
> Burma-Shave. (Verse 53)

And these from 1952:

> His
> Tomato
> Was the mushy type
> Until his beard
> Grew over-ripe
> Burma-Shave. (Verse 54)

> He asked
> His kitten
> To pet and purr
> She eyed his puss
> And screamed "What fur!"
> Burma-Shave. (Verse 55)

Many women today would see these as degrading, although they weren't seen that way during the years they were put up as Burma-Shave signs.

Or this one, which appeared in 1937:

> The cannibals
> Took just one view
> And said
> He looks
> Too nice to stew.
> Burma-Shave. (Verse 56)

It probably would not work for today's Americans.

Even some of the jingoistic titles might anger some people today, like this one from 1942:

> Let's make Hitler
> And Hirohito
> Look as sick
> As old Benito.
> Buy defense bonds.
> Burma-Shave. (Verse 57)

And definitely,

> Slap
> The
> Jap
> With
> Iron scrap
> Burma-Shave. (Verse 58)

would trouble a lot of people today, even if the United States was at war with Japan. In 1951, a time when movie Westerns were so popular, this one was put up, but it easily would prove objectionable today:

> Another
> Red skin
> Bit the dust
> When pa tried
> What these signs discussed.
> Burma-Shave. (Verse 59)

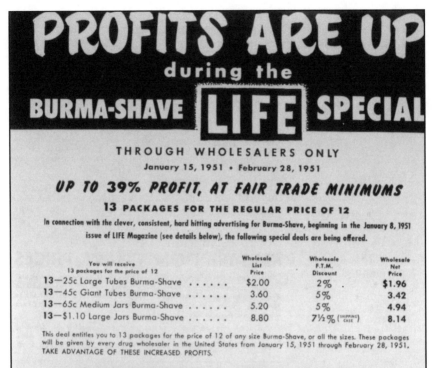

Profits may have been up for jobbers and wholesalers during the time this 1951 offer came out, but Burma-Vita was probably not doing as well as it wanted.

Because of modern violence, this one from 1952 would not work today:

> She put
> A bullet
> Thru his hat
> But he's had
> Closer shaves than that
> Burma-Shave. (Verse 60)

Had any of these been deemed the least bit improper, they would never have been used.

Chapter 12

BLUE AND TABOO

The Odells were very choosy about which rhymes were used. But they received all kinds of rhymes during their contests. Some were funny but off-color; some were shocking and might elicit a one-time nervous laugh; and some were simply odd and/or incomprehensible.

"Dad was careful," said Leonard in the video *The Signs and Rhymes of Burma-Shave,* "He'd say, 'No, that jingle might offend somebody.'"

So some jingles were never used:

> The other woman
> In his life
> Said
> "Go back home
> And scratch your wife."
> Burma-Shave.

And

> The wife
> Of bristly
> Brushmug Zaymer
> Bought twin beds.
> Who can blame her?
> Burma-Shave.

MUSA Online on the Internet wrote, "Some had to be censored, like this one which was never used:

"My man won't shave,"
Said Hazel Huz,
"But
I don't worry.
Dora's does."
Burma-Shave.

Others came close to being censored but were used:

Substitutes
Can let you down
Quicker
Than a
Strapless gown
Burma-Shave. (Verse 61)

Others were very obviously improper, and were submitted to the Burma-Shave contests, but were not accepted for publication:

Eighty years old
Never more chipper
Beard got caught
In stripper's zipper.
Burma-Shave.

Have you heard
The one about the man
On the flying trapeze
Who caught
His wife in the act?
Burma-Shave.

Casanova's whiskers
Gave he-man look
But they cooked his goose
When he
Goosed his cook.
Burma-Shave.

You can't
Get milk
From any bull
Like Burma-Shave
There is no pull!
Burma-Shave.

Mom's Iceman
Has another route
Since dad
Discovered
All about
Burma-Shave.

Hand out
For
Feel
Seldom
On wheel
Burma-Shave.

A sure way to spoil
A dreamy waltz
Is for me to feel
That her charms
Are false.
Burma-Shave.

Prospectors find
Their gold
With muscle
Gold-diggers use
A well-shaped bustle.
Burma-Shave.

My gal clapped
Her hands
When she felt my face
But when she felt my hands
She slapped my face.
Burma-Shave.

These were obviously improper during their time—most would also
be deemed improper for advertising today—and there are those which are
not in this book which were bluer. The Odells never considered using any
of these, simply because they wanted a company and a product associated
with cleanliness and purity, and the off-color rhymes didn't fit into their
moral structure.

Burma-Shave Signs . . . or Imposters?

Some Burma-Shave jingles thought to be original, like these never-
used ones below, probably weren't, said Clinton B. Odell:

A nut
At the wheel
A peach at his right
A curve ahead
Salad tonight
Burma-Shave.

If wife shuns
Your fond embrace
Don't shoot
The iceman
Feel your face.
Burma-Shave.

Diplomacy
Is to do
And say
The nastiest things
In the nicest way
Burma-Shave.

Don't take to
Cutting in and out
Stay in line
When you're
In doubt
Burma-Shave.

Doing sixty
Safety cheaters
Turn miles
Into Kill-O-meters
Burma-Shave.

If you pass
On the yellow line
Hope the funeral's
Yours
Not mine
Burma-Shave.

Chapter 13

UNUSUAL USES FOR THE SIGNS

urma-Shave signs had uses the creators hadn't considered. One was as a scratching post for cows and horses. Originally the bottom of the Burma-Shave board was five feet high, which allowed horses to reach them and rub against them. Many signs were tilted, broken or completely destroyed by animals before Burma-Vita changed the bottom height of the boards to seven feet.

Another use for the Burma-Shave signs was as a reading tool. As Buck Buchanan wrote in the June 1989 issue of *Trailer Life* magazine, "'Reading Burma-Shave signs,' was the quick-and-easy answer that brought a smile to Miss Rickman's face on the first day of first grade in Boyd, Texas, when she asked, 'Where on earth did you learn to read like that at your age?'

"There was never any doubt in my mind as to where I acquired that knowledge, along with an eagerness for reading that sticks with me to this day. It came from staring through the dust-covered windshield of an old Model T, as Mom and I read those signs together. There was plenty of time to read them, at thirty miles per hour, Dad's maximum speed with or without the trailer.

"My wife, Tilly, asked just yesterday, 'Why don't they put the info from those historical markers on little signs, like Burma-Shave used to do? Then we could read them without stopping.' Good question."

Burma-Shave was also good for salving injuries. A man from Minneapolis said in Ann Landers' syndicated column that he was a hospital corpsman with the First Marine Division during the battle to secure Okinawa. "Most of us carried Burma-Shave in our first-aid supplies. It was an excellent treatment for white phosphorous burns. It cooled the burn, soothed the pain and extinguished any phosphorous that might still be burning. Burma-Shave made a very positive contribution to World War II."

Also, the Burma-Shave signs saved at least one man's life during a Midwest blizzard.

"I had an old Model A in the early thirties in North Dakota before any of these newfangled fancy roads came about," said a man who wishes to remain anonymous. "I was a young man and maybe a little bit arrogant because I had this car and not a lot of young people had cars in those days. I thought I was invincible, too, like a lot of young people do. At any rate, I left home early in the morning and didn't pay much attention to the weather. It was late November, and, as I drove, I saw there were some black clouds in the sky, but I didn't pay much attention to them. I was heading a few miles away to spark one of the local beauties, and I had shaved real close, and I had probably even used Burma-Shave because I remember that I liked Burma-Shave and thought that the signs were not only funny, but they were true, too. My favorite one came quite a bit later:

> Remember this
> If you'd
> Be spared
> Trains don't whistle
> Because they're scared
> Burma-Shave. (Verse 62)

"At any rate, Leora's house was just a few miles away, and I wasn't worrying too much about anything, just thinking about her a little bit and what we were going to do, and as I was driving over this country road a few snowflakes started drifting down from the sky, and it didn't take long until there were more and more of them, and you can guess what happened next. The wind picked up, and more snow came, and there I was caught in a full-fledged blizzard. Before I knew what had happened, I couldn't see the road, and I plowed into a ditch and got stuck. Nothing I could do would get me out. I hadn't dressed very warmly because I had only been going a few miles, and suddenly it got cold, real damn cold. I knew I was in big trouble.

66

Nowadays they tell you to stay with the car if you get stuck, but in those days, we didn't have any kind of information like that. Plus those old heaters weren't worth a doggone. So I started walking. It didn't take me long to realize that was a mistake, but by then, the snow had covered my footsteps, and I couldn't make it back to the car. There'd been this story of a schoolgirl who froze to death protecting her younger sister during a blizzard, and I started thinking about that. I couldn't see diddly, and I thought the good Lord was going to take me away.

"But then I stumbled into a sign. By that time I didn't know if I was in the middle of a pasture or if I was in someone's yard. I walked around to the front of the sign, and sure enough, it was one of those Burma-Shave signs. Those signs were so much fun and so important, I guess, that people always knew where they were located. And I knew where this one was: on the main road next to Leora's folks' driveway. It was the fourth sign in the series, and said "When he died." [the entire verse is:

> Shaving brush
> Was like
> Old Rover
> When he died
> He died all over
> Burma-Shave. (Verse 63)]

"First I shivered because I thought maybe somebody was trying to tell me something. Then, let me tell you, I stood there and hugged it, and even thought about kissing it. It made me think, too, if I shouldn't be getting married, lucky as I'd been.

"It didn't take me long to find the next two signs, and then Leora's driveway. Somebody had taken the horses out, I found out later, and was going to look for me, so I had a clear trail to their house. I almost didn't make it. I was sure tired, and numb, and I thought about just curling up there on the road for a little nap. But I made it to the house, and they were sure glad to see me. Lost part of two fingers, but you could say Burma-Shave signs saved my life. I thought it would really have been nice if that sign I saw was part of one that had to do with safety, or something like that, but it wasn't."

Don Boxmeyer wrote in the *St. Paul Pioneer Press* that "About seventeen years ago I visited Allan Odell in his Twin Cities home. I asked if

67

he'd saved any of his originals and he said, sadly, that he had sent the last complete set to the Smithsonian Institution.

"Not so, said Allan's wife, Grace. She reminded him that when they built the house, they saved money by installing their own wooden floor in the attic. The place was wall-to-wall in Burma-Shave wisdom, a floorful of country advice to live by, laid out in sequence."

Original Burma-Shave boards show up all across the country from time to time; some are even put alongside roads to evoke the old nostalgia. Occasionally they can be found at swap meets and antique shops, as they have become collector items.

A study conducted by the University of Pennsylvania reported that no phenomenon more reliably slowed down speeders than a set of Burma-Shave signs.

Or gave them as much fun.

Burma-Shave's logo became familiar to millions of Americans during the heyday of the company, from 1926 to 1963.

Chapter 14

BURMA-VITA'S OTHER ADVERTISING

urma-Shave also used other advertising methods besides signs; in fact, in the late 1940s, Burma-Vita quit using the signs for a while. In 1951, Burma-Shave contracted with a cartoonist to push their product: "Each ad will feature a new, original cartoon by the famous and popular LICHTY—illustrating one of Burma-Shave's clever roadsign jingles. Your customers will watch for these cartoons—chuckle over them—and ask for Burma-Shave." These cartoons were presented in *Life* magazine.

One for January 8 had the jingle:

> Since hubby
> Tried
> That substitute
> He's 1/3 man
> And 2/3 brute
> Burma-Shave. (Verse 64)

The cartoon showed a man at the left in the bathroom cursing, while his wife holds a crying baby, and a young child crying beside her. The ad read "You've chuckled for years at the Burma-Shave jingles along the highways—but have you ever treated yourself to a Burma-Shave shave? Once you discover how good your face feels afterwards, you'll be a Burma-Shave enthusiast for life!"

Two weeks later, the jingle read:

> If your peach
> Keeps out
> Of reach
> Better practice
> What we preach
> Burma-Shave. (Verse 65)

and showed a man chasing a woman around an office desk. The ad reads "Frankly, we don't believe all the millions of Burma-Shave users buy it for the reason suggested above. We suspect most of 'em like it because it leaves their faces feeling so doggone good. That's why you'll like it too!"

The February 5 edition had:

> When
> Super-shaved
> Remember pard
> You'll still get slapped
> But not so hard
> Burma-Shave. (Verse 66)

and shows a woman slapping a man, but with love-hearts resulting instead of painful stars.

Two weeks after that, the cartoon showed a hobo walking down a railroad track, and the rhyme said:

> Men
> Who have to
> Travel light
> Find the handy tube
> Just right.
> Burma-Shave. (Verse 67)

The ad read, "After the shave is over, that's when you can tell how good a shaving cream really is. When you see how happy your face feels after being Burma-Shaved, you'll joyously join the millions who use Burma-Shave regularly!"

Burma-Vita took their Burma-Shave advertising campaign to *Life* magazine in 1951.

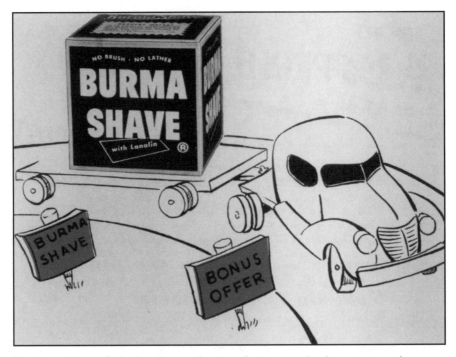

The success of Burma-Vita's advertising gave Americans the impression that the company was a large cor-
poration, when, in fact, no more than thirty-five people ever worked at the Minneapolis plant at a time.

In May 1951, *Life* ran:

> To kiss
> A mug
> That's like a cactus
> Takes more nerve
> Than it does practice
> Burma-Shave. (Verse 68)

and shows a scratchy-bearded man on a sofa, and his girlfriend sitting far
away, arms crossed, wearing a baseball catcher's mask. Curiously enough, an
undated cartoon done by Lichty that appeared in *Life* has a very slightly different jingle—and thus the cartoon—than the signs did. The signs read:

Candidate says
Campaign
Confusing.
Babies kiss me since
I've been using
Burma-Shave. (Verse 69)

Lichty changed "babies" to "BABES" in the *Life* cartoon, and shows a politician surrounded by women who are kissing him. Whether this was an accident, or a misreading, or done on purpose, is not clear.

Burma-Shave products were advertised heavily in druggists' and pharmaceutical magazines, contest magazines, and many more print outlets. Some of those advertisements accompany the text of this book.

Burma-Shave was not shy about letting people know how it was doing. (Today it would be considered a trade secret, perhaps.) And of course Burma-Shave advertised their own coups through, what else? Their signs. The first one, in 1929, read simply,

Two
Hundred
Thousand
Men
Use
Burma-Shave. (Verse 70)

In 1930, it was 500,000, and then 600,000; in 1931, 800,000; in 1933, one of the signs proudly read,

The millionth man
Has joined
Our ranks
Of happy shavers
Many thanks
Burma-Shave. (Verse 71)

By 1935, the number of Burma-Shave users had risen to two million, and a year later, three million. Astoundingly, this huge growth was accomplished during the darkest days of the Great Depression; perhaps men look-

In addition to advertising by means of the six signs by the side of America's roads, Burma-Vita also took the more usual routes, as this ad from *Central Pharmaceutical Journal* from 1950 shows. Burma-Vita always gave their jobbers and dealers bonuses of extra merchandise for ordering.

Burma-Shave also portrayed, very effectively, what would happen to the man who didn't shave his chin. This streetcar card was one of a series used mainly during World War II, when signs couldn't be put up along roads due to wartime restrictions on gasoline and rubber tires.

ing for work felt they looked better shaved, and had a better chance of getting a job; or maybe Burma-Shave's concept that shaved men were better looking and more liked by women, had finally caught on.

By 1947 there were six million men shaving with Burma-Shave.

Burma-Shave was also advertised through streetcar cards, mostly during World War II, when roadside signs couldn't be set up or properly maintained because of wartime restrictions in using vehicles.

There is little doubt, however, that it was the six signs of advertising that were most effective for Burma-Shave.

Chapter 15

ONCE UPON A BURMA-SHAVE SIGN

ractically everybody who grew up from the late 1920s through the middle 1950s has a remembrance or story about Burma-Shave and the signs because they and the signs came to maturity during those years, along with cars. Today's youth would be hard pressed to understand the importance of the introduction of the automobile into society and how it altered mobility and travel.

But these stories are more than mere nostalgic remembrances; they are portals back into a time when, everybody who lived then is sure, that life was simpler, less dangerous and more fun.

When Ben and Agnes R. of Minnesota went for a trip out west, they took their young school-age son along. Having been a schoolteacher herself, Agnes understood the value of education, but she also knew how to implement it in her son's life in a fun way. For arithmetic, their son had to total the amount the family spent on gas and meals, and figure out their mileage by long division. For reading and writing, he was required to read all the Burma-Shave signs they saw, and write each one in a notebook.

Ellen wrote on-line that, "I remember reading the Burma-Shave signs when we'd go on vacation, and they were a lot of fun. I just wish I could remember some of them. My brother and I would squabble in the back seat until Dad would have us start watching for the signs, and we'd squabble over which side of the car to look out of."

In 1951, Burma-Vita tried another unique method of advertising, using cartoons by Lichty to spread their word every two weeks in *Life* magazine. Note the distinctive Lichty rounded-stroke cartooning design in the head at the bottom.

One woman wrote that for her and her boyfriend at the time (later her husband), the signs actually backfired. "Clem was always kind of a contrary person, which I can say with comfort now that he has passed on, I suppose. When we were dating, and we'd come on one of those Burma-Shave signs that warned us not to do something, why, he'd up and do it.
"Like

> Don't take
> A curve
> At 60-per.
> We hate to lose
> A customer
> Burma-Shave. (Verse 72)

77

When he saw that, he'd try to find a curve that he could go fast around, and I don't know if he drove sixty, but he drove fast. Or

> You can't reach 80
> Hale and hearty
> By driving 80
> Home from
> The party.
> Burma-Shave. (Verse 73)

Later he told me that he had gone out first and checked if he could drive eighty on that stretch [like he did] when we went home from that party that one time, or go that fast around a curve, because he didn't want anyone to get hurt, and he just wanted to impress me. I don't know if that's true. But that's how he was."

Mark Edwards wrote that when he was a kid, his parents used to take them to Raccoon Lake, in Indiana. "Along the way we would always look for the signs. Now, I never knew that they were ads, but I remember that they were clever rhymes, and certainly great ways to keep young kids quiet while traveling. We . . . always looked forward to the signs, even though I don't remember a word from any of the signs."

Les Albert said that when he was about thirteen, he saw a Burma-Shave sign that puzzled him:

> You will click
> Like a Bolshevik
> If you don't use
> Burma-Shave.

(The actual verse read:)

> With glamour girls
> You'll never click
> Bewhiskered like
> A Bolshevik.
> Burma-Shave. (Verse 74)

"I never asked anyone what it meant, and it wasn't until years later that I understood the sign. It is the only Burma-Shave sign that I remember although I saw many of them as a kid."

Mary E. of Idaho wrote that one of the funniest things she ever saw involved a set of Burma-Shave signs. "For whatever reason, someone had taken a set of the signs and had exchanged some of the signs with one of the old rhymes. Or maybe the guys who put up the signs thought it would be funny to have a set where two rhymes worked together. Or maybe they ran out of signs all the way out here and didn't know it until they had put out most of them in that new set. Anyhoo, what you had was a set of the six signs, but two of them were from one rhyme, and three of them from another one, and the most amazing thing of all was that they worked! They made a bizarre sort of sense together! I wish I could remember which signs they were, and what they said, but I don't. It might have been:

> It's best for
> One who hits
> The bottle
> To let another
> Use the Throttle
> Burma-Shave. (Verse 75)

along with another rhyme. I surely wish I could remember which ones they were, because they gave us a lot of pleasure that I think that little company never planned on giving. I know I wrote the whole thing down one time, after the next new set had been put up, but I guess I lost it. Funniest thing I've ever seen, I think."

Judge Glen Ashman, host of the Dixie States Forum on Delphi, said "I know that as a young kid I used to count them (and try to outcount a sister). It was a travel game rather like different color cars or how many different state license plates [you could find]."

S. Monroe drove semi tractor-trailers for more than twenty years, and never did see any Burma-Shave signs, he said, but then he started in 1974. "I actually used to go to roadside antique and junk stores looking for them. Seems like they all rusted away. I have seen them nailed to the walls of bars, old license plate style but can't remember where."

When Virginia H. went to visit her grandmother in Ohio, she said she saw Burma-Shave signs all over the place. "I don't remember seeing them anywhere else. Here is one I remember particularly. I am sufficiently evil to quote it to those to whom it applies:

> In this vale
> Of pain and sin
> Your head grows bald
> But not your chin.
> Burma-Shave.

[The actual verse:]

> Within this vale
> Of toil
> And sin
> Your head grows bald
> But not your chin—use
> Burma-Shave. (Verse 76)

She said there was a particularly gory one that was much loved by her brother, but she couldn't remember the rhyme. "Something like:"

> She reached out
> To wave too far.
> Her arm went home
> In another car.
> Burma-Shave.

The actual verse:

> Don't stick
> Your elbow
> Out so far
> It might go home
> In another car.
> Burma-Shave. (Verse 77)

Even though people can't remember the exact words, they certainly can remember the concepts Burma-Shave was espousing.

Joanne Omanj said her family drove back and forth across the country four times when she was growing up, from one military base assignment to the next, in the late 1940s and early 1950s. "I'd be sprawled in the back seat with my comic books unresponsive to exhortations to look at the beautiful scenery, but whenever somebody announced a Burma-Shave series I sprang to attention. They all had five signs and a signoff 'Burma-Shave' at the end. I remember them as red with white lettering. They weren't very frequent; maybe two sets in an entire day of driving (about 350 miles was a good run in those two-lane highway days.)

"Some faves:

> He was right, dead right
> As he sped along
> And just as dead
> As if he'd been wrong.
> Burma-Shave.

> The rain it falleth equally
> Upon the just and unjust fella
> But more upon the just, because
> The unjust stole the just's umbrella.
> Burma-Shave.

("This last one may be an ersatz memory inserted in my Burma-Shave signs mental file from a later epoch.")

> That she
> Could cook
> He had his doubts
> Until she creamed
> His bristle sprouts.
> Burma-Shave. (Verse 78)

William Childress wrote in *Geico Direct* magazine, "Ah, yes, how many of us can remember those Burma-Shave signs . . .

"'Wake up, wake up, they're more a-comin'!' My little brother's elbow punctuated the urgency of his yell. Aroused from my car-induced sleep just in time to look out the windows and see:

Santa's
Whiskers
Need no trimmin
He kisses kids
Not the wimmin
Burma-Shave. (Verse 79)

"It was 1947, and we were leaving red-dirt Oklahoma for the promised land of California. The road was a two-lane blacktop called Route 66, and by far the most entertaining thing we . . . saw along this fabled highway were little white-on-red signs that bore jingles for something we wouldn't need for years—shaving cream.

Cheek to cheek
They meant to be
The lights went out
And so did he
He needed
Burma-Shave. (Verse 80)

"How we doubled up and howled at those signs. Now that we little shavers have become real shavers, my brother and I and millions of other Americans mourn the passing of the cheery little signs. 'I'm convinced I learned to read from Burma-Shave signs,' says my druggist, who is fifty-some and severely stubbled most days. 'In the 1930s dad traveled a lot, and sometimes I went with him. Those signs were everywhere then . . . '"

Writer Walter Higbee said if you ask someone under forty to complete a Burma-Shave rhyme, you will get no response. "Ask anyone over fifty to complete it, and you will elicit a smile and hear, 'Burma-Shave!'"

"Yes, there was a time in the 1930s and 1940s when Burma-Shave signs covered the highways and country roads of the country. They were erected on a series of wooden cross pieces and spaced about a hundred feet apart, just right for reading when traveling thirty-five to forty-five miles an hour. Kids in the back seat would chant in unison when one of the following was spotted as Dad tooled down the road in his Model A:

Does your husband
Misbehave?
Grunt and grumble
Rant and rave?
Shoot the brute some
Burma-Shave. (Verse 28)

"It was a lot of fun to see who could shout the last line, 'Burma-Shave,' the loudest."

Marylaine Block wrote in her weekly column, "My Word's Worth," of August 1995: "Our weekly migrations were before the interstate highways came along. We had two-lane traffic, with Burma-Shave signs facing each lane. For those of you born too late to know what I'm talking about, these were brief verses spread over four or five [actually six] signs, ending with the advertising pitch, as in:

Around the curve
Lickety split
Beautiful car
Wasn't it?
Buy
Burma-Shave. (Verse 81)

"The child on the right was assigned to read aloud the forward Burma-Shave signs. But the older child on the left had the awesome responsibility of reading the backward Burma-Shave signs, sticking them into short-term memory, reconstructing them, and reciting them in the correct order."

Walter Higbee wrote in "Senior Joys," "The last Burma-Shave sign was taken down in 1963 [actually 1965]. They had been a part of Americana for more than thirty years. It was said that travel on interstates and the more hectic pace of living were responsible for their demise. Too bad, really. Just imagine what gales of laughter would issue forth from the back seat from your kids and mine if they read something like:

Listen birds
These signs
Cost money.
Rest awhile,
But don't get funny!
Burma-Shave."

Dale Murphy of Florida said "When it was announced that the signs were being discontinued, I took the ones that were on our fenceposts and took 'em down and put 'em in the barn." Theirs had said:

If harmony
Is what
You crave,
Then get
A tuba
Burma-Shave. (Verse 24)

William Childress, in *Geigo Direct*, wrote, "But for folks who still recall the grand old days of auto travel—when the wind in our hair as we stuck our heads out,made even a twenty-mile trip an adventure in fun—the Burma-Shave signs will always grace the meadows of our minds." (Courtesy of the Stearns County Historical Society, St. Cloud, Minnesota)

William Childress said, "There was a time, in the not-too-distant past, when driving was a pleasure in spite of far-apart gas stations and synthetic rubber tires. These journeys—whether cross country or town-to-town jaunts—were enhanced by bright little signs by the side of highways all over America—signs containing jingles that made us giggle, or think, or laugh out loud:

> He married Grace
> With scratchy face
> He only
> Got one day
> Of Grace!
> Burma-Shave. (Verse 82)

There is much wishful thinking that some signs have missed the grim reaper's scythe. Don Boxmeyer wrote in the *Pioneer Press,* "Even today, something or someone gives the legend a bump every five or ten years, creating a new interest in Burma-Shave. Just a few years back, someone got the rights to print some of the most popular Burma Shave jingles on pine boards to sell as art objects."

Childress added, "But for folks who still recall the grand old days of auto travel—when the wind in our hair as we stuck our heads out, made even a twenty-mile trip an adventure in fun—the Burma-Shave signs will always grace the meadows of our minds.

"As for those of you who are too young to have known that rousing, rollicking verse by the side of the road, you have my utmost sympathy."

Chapter 16

WHY DID BURMA-SHAVE SIGNS WORK?

A flip view would say that the signs worked simply because they worked, but one thing is certain: the time was right, with everything perfect for the signs to work. This does not detract from the Odells' hard work to make their company successful; it simply means that the apples were ripe to be plucked, and they plucked them.

The reasons the signs worked are many:

First, the increasing popularity of the automobile. "People were just starting to travel across the country in automobiles," said Joe Blackstock. The signs relieved boredom in the car, he said. "A bunch of kids crammed in a car all had something to look for: the next Burma-Shave signs:

> Riot at
> Drug store
> Calling all cars
> 100 customers
> 99 jars
> Burma-Shave. (Verse 83)

In 1920, one passenger car was registered for every thirteen Americans; ten years later it had nearly doubled to two cars registered for every eleven Americans, which showed the increase in the popularity of the automobile.

When Burma-Shave came out, not only did Burma-Vita have to find means to market their product, but it had to train its customers also. Directions for use on the tube or jar read, "No lather. Wash face thoroughly with soap and water. Leave beard moist. Spread on Burma-Shave with fingers. After spreading, pat, don't rub. Allow a minute for Burma-Shave to set. Shave."

Americans were willing to purchase cars, and families even broke the old Puritan taboo against personal debt. The high cost and the care of cars could keep people in debt for most of their productive lives. Yet car ownership was a bondage willingly assumed. A small-town banker observed in 1925 in *We Americans*, a 1975 compilation of the National Geographic Society: "The paramount ambition of the average man a few years ago was to own a home and have a bank account. The ambition of the same man today is to own a car . . . whatever the reason, the result is . . . debt, debt, debt, for a costly article that depreciates very rapidly and has an insatiable appetite for money." And yet he concluded, "I still drive one myself. I must keep up with the procession."

Behind this advancing wave came a new array of industries. The Americans whose livelihoods were directly linked to the automobile included owners and employees of garages, service stations, auto parts stores, roadside restaurants, and the "tourist cabins" which eventually acquired sophistication and became motels. The Automobile Age also generated a formidable expansion of the petroleum, rubber, steel and glass industries, which led the way to the boom of the 1920s. With more people involved in automobile industries, concepts involving autos—like the Burma-Shave signs— became lodged in people's consciousnesses.

87

Federal, state, and local government gave priority to highway construction, forever transforming the national landscape, and, in doing so, set up conditions for Burma-Shave signs to be placed beside roads.

Second, Burma-Shave signs worked because of the state of advertising itself. There was little competition for Burma-Shave in the way of roadsign ads.

The book *We Americans* said that early advertising was just starting to come into its own. "The creativity of advertising men soared on the wings of enticing automotive copy. Crude facts of horsepower and gear ratios became less important than the intangible ego satisfactions of ownership. 'There's a savor . . . about that car,' ran a trend-setting ad of 1926, 'of laughter and lilt and light—a hint of old loves—and saddle and quirt. It's a brawny thing, yet a graceful thing for the sweep o' the Avenue.' Hidden desires for status, power, sexuality, and rebelliousness were coaxed into the open and promised gratification through the properly styled machine. Like movies, auto ads pandered to the fantasies of men and women caught up in a mechanized world. Paradoxically, the ads promised individuality through mass consumption."

All this advertising attention about the automobile created not only a great deal of interest in autos, but was different from all other advertising of the day, targeted towards scaring people. Don Boxmeyer, a columnist for the *Pioneer Press* wrote that "The catchy little couplets caught on immediately, and the orders for Burma-Shave rolled in. The secret was that the signs were light-hearted and never mean at a time when big advertisers were trying to scare people into buying Absorbine Jr. for their toes and Feenament for their bowels."

Burma-Shave, with its curious and enjoyable and funny jingles, spoke to consumers in a way that they had never quite been spoken to before and grabbed people's attention:

> The time
> To start
> A real dispute
> Is when you're
> Offered a substitute.
> Burma-Shave. (Verse 84)

A third reason Burma-Shave signs worked was because America was rural. That meant long uncluttered spaces where the signs could be set out so people could see them; poorer roads, which required slower travel; a group of people for whom almost any car travel was an adventure; and all the nostalgic, positive things a person can say about the rural past.

Fourth, Burma-Shave signs worked because America was different then than it is today, in all the best senses. Life was slower-paced, and people were less harried, and could take time to look for Burma-Shave signs, and read them. Grace Odell said, "It was just different, a simpler time, an easier life, and yet we had so much."

The fifth reason Burma-Shave signs worked was because they interested the readers. Kippy Burns, vice president communications of the Outdoor Advertising Association of America said the jingles engaged the readers. "That's what really good outdoor advertising does yet today."

Every traveler who grew up in the 1930s, 1940s, and 1950s, remembers the excitement of coming onto another set of Burma-Shave signs, and reading them aloud one-by-one (sometimes backwards from the far side of the road):

> A chin
> Where barbed wire
> Bristles stand
> Is bound to be
> A no ma'am's land
> Burma-Shave. (Verse 85)

> Heaven's
> Latest
> Neophyte
> Signalled left
> Then turned right.
> Burma-Shave. (Verse 86)

Everyone knew the words on the final sign and enjoyed shouting them in unison: Burma-Shave! That immediate product recognition was an incredible advertising coup.

Mary W. of Iowa said when she was a kid, she and her sister were told to watch for Burma-Shave signs when they went with their dad as he sold Fuller Brushes. "Our mother had died by then, and we spent a lot of hours in the car with daddy. When we got too antsy, daddy would ask us to read the Burma-Shave signs aloud to him. Mine were easy . . . they were on my side of the road. Sherry's were harder, because she had to read the back-wards one. They were on the other side of the road, so she had to memorize them all backwards, and then read them back to us.

"Sometimes she would start reading backwards, beginning with 'Burma-Shave!' and we'd have to figure out what the rhyme said. Or some-times she'd pretend she was reading the signs, but she would make up anoth-er poem that sounded like a Burma-Shave rhyme. She was always quick with making up stuff, and especially rhymes. For a while she got paid to do it on radio. Anyway, daddy would laugh and laugh at some of her poems and say, 'That's the best Burma-Shave sign I've heard in months.'" Later he told us he figured it out pretty quick by looking in the rear-view mirror. He couldn't always read the words Sherry was supposed to be saying, but he could see how many words were on the signs. But he never said anything when we were kids. 'Anything that would make us laugh at that time was good,'" he always said.

The sixth reason for Burma-Shave sign success was the positiveness of the signs. As Burma-Shave signs began appearing, the United States became mired in the debilitating Great Depression. Faces were long everywhere, and life was hard. Into this darkness came the light and uplifting Burma-Shave signs.

As was written on MUSA on-line, "Burma-Shave was a brilliant idea. America in the 1930s was torn by the Great Depression. Spirits were low. But here was a little company brightening the countryside with cheer-ful rhymes.

Grace Odell said, "Positive thinking is the best thing you can have. It works. Everything was positive in the signs. We just wanted to have it fun for people to drive, and they did. Allan had the idea of something that was uplifting and made people laugh, and I think it really truly helped the dri-ving. People were always looking for those little signs."

The seventh reason was the roads themselves. People could not travel fast on them. MUSA on-line said: "Few things recall America's lost innocence better than those old Burma-Shave signs that flourished in a time of family picnics and quiet Sundays at Grandma's house. . . . Can you imagine trying to enjoy those jingles in today's freeway traffic? We can barely read the exit numbers. And if you see an advertisement, it will be shouting at you, threatening you with underarm wetness or some other dreadful ailment. It won't contain the serene good humor of Burma-Shave's poets."

The eighth reason Burma-Shave signs worked was more subtle—the bearded tradition, beards, and how women felt about them. Joe Blackstock said many American men were bearded at the time, which many women didn't like, and some of the verses actually helped convert men:

> To get
> Away from
> Hairy apes
> Ladies jump
> From fire escapes
> Burma-Shave. (Verse 87)

A much higher percentage of the male population wore beards than is common today, as is shown by this photo of the Fuchs brothers, of Cold Spring, Minnesota, ca. 1890. (Courtesy of the Stearns County Historical Society of St. Cloud, Minnesota)

In the 1920s, the United States was quite a different place from today, said Blackstock. For one thing, a much higher percentage of the male population had beards than they do today, hangovers from when their fathers and grandfathers had beards. Blackstock said, "A lot of men were still wearing a lot of hair on their faces in those days. Many women didn't like the beards on their husbands and boyfriends."

The ninth reason was the company's wholesome reputation: From the start, Burma-Shave was predicated on old-fashioned American virtues of kindness, gentleness, and honesty—beginning with Clinton Odell's kind gesture of giving twenty-five dollars to a hurting stranger. Clinton wanted a gentle company with a wholesome reputation, and that's what he got, and what the American people appreciated.

Tenth, Burma-Shave signs worked because the signs were a type of advertising never seen before, with jingles poking fun at Burma-Shave and Burma-Vita, which large and more serious companies didn't do (and rarely do today,) and jingles that were short, peppy, humorous, and fun.

In 1942:

> If you don't know
> Whose signs
> These are
> You can't have
> Driven very far
> Burma-Shave. (Verse 88)

And in 1945:

> This is not
> A clever verse.
> I tried
> And tried
> But just got worse
> Burma-Shave. (Verse 89)

Also 1945, with airplanes becoming more common in the United States:

> 'Twould be
> More fun
> To go by air
> If we could put
> These signs up there
> Burma-Shave. (Verse 90)

1947:

> As you drive
> Play this game
> Construct
> A jingle
> With this name
> Burma-Shave. (Verse 91)

And then in 1948:

> I've read
> These signs
> Since just a kid
> Now that I shave
> I'm glad I did
> Burma-Shave. (Verse 92)

One of their oddest rhymes was this one from 1949:

> Just this once
> And just for fun
> We'll let you finish
> What we've begun
> ??? (Verse 93)

Also in 1949,

> Old Dobbin
> Reads these signs
> Each day.
> You see, he gets
> His corn that way
> Burma-Shave. (Verse 94)

Signs were sometimes corny—

> Cautious rider
> To her reckless dear
> "Let's have less bull
> And lots more steer"
> Burma-Shave. (Verse 95)

and witty—

> Past
> Schoolhouses
> Take it slow.
> Let the little
> Shavers grow
> Burma-Shave. (Verse 96)

Burma-Shave was successful for the definable reasons listed, but for indefinable reasons as well:

Online at a site called "Signage," they wrote, "Riding in a car was enjoyable when you could do it as a wide-eyed innocent in the back seat. The best of those times was spent looking for Burma-Shave signs along the road. The ditties, though trite, always drew laughs. With apologies (to Odells):

In the Burma-Vita warehouse, signs wait to be taken out and erected. The one shown was Allan Odell's favorite out of all the 600 or so jingles that were put up on signs across America.

A clever man
Known as Odell
Never littered the highway
With messages
From hell.
Burma-Shave. John McNeely,
Columbus Dispatch.

Don Boxmeyer wrote in the *Pioneer Press*, that "The Burma-Shave legend is a beloved part of Americana that went over the hill about the time the freeways got here. Beginning in the 1920s and lasting for almost four decades, Burma-Shave couplets on wooded plaques touted brushless shaving cream from coast to coast.

"Burma-Shave became the national philosophy, common sense that rhymed." And worked entertaining Americans for nearly forty years.

Chapter 17

ARCHEOLOGY IN WORDS

*O*ne of the most fascinating aspects of the Burma-Shave jingles is their window into another era of life. Each Burma-Shave jingle is a layer, a strata back into another time, showing what people were thinking about, how they thought, what they liked and disliked, and what they feared.

Take this jingle from 1931:

> The one horse shay
> Has had its day
> So has the brush
> And lather way
> Use
> Burma-Shave. (Verse 97)

The one-horse shay, an open-sided, roofed carriage, had been a popular and common method of horse transportation for many years (the "shay" was more properly called a "chaise"); this little ditty calls up some common literature of the time, taught all across the United States, the poem about the one-horse shay ("The Deacon's Masterpiece, or The Wonderful One-Hoss Shay," by Oliver Wendell Holmes). This ditty harkens back to a time in the United States when memorizing poetry was almost a reflex in schools.

This Burma-Shave rhyme also points to a time when more of the country was in sync with everybody else in the country than today—there was a more general school curriculum taught, for instance, which allowed some of these Burma-Shave ditties and their references to be recognized by nearly everybody, which added to their success.

The one-horse shay rhyme also could be read to mean that America revered poetry and literature then more than today.

A 1932 rhyme,

> For painting
> Cow-shed
> Barn or fence
> That shaving brush
> Is just immense.
> Burma-Shave. (Verse 98)

reflected the buildings on the landscape of America at the time; though the number of farmers had begun to decrease, and would decrease a great deal more during the coming Great Depression, farming, with the cowshed, barn, and fence, still dominated the American landscape.

Perhaps it was a 1932 trend, but another verse,

> When the jar
> Is empty
> Wife begins to sing
> "For spices, jam, and jelly
> That jar is just the thing."
> Burma-Shave. (Verse 99)

also reflected a time when women stayed at home, and one of their major duties was to can jams and jellies. Canning jars were at a premium, especially during the Depression. This is not a rhyme that could comfortably grace roadsides today, because it would simply be too foreign.

A 1933 jingle speaks for itself:

> Shaving brush
> Don't you cry,
> You'll be a
> Shoe dauber
> By and by.
> Burma-Shave. (Verse 100)

reflecting the need to daub shoe polish on shoes. Additionally, this jingle is a play on a children's lullaby ("Hush Little Baby"), with some of the same words: "Don't you cry . . ."

Several jingles pointed out worsening economic conditions in the country as the Great Depression began to deepen, beginning with this one in 1934:

> Tho living costs
> Are upward bound
> Four bits
> Still buys
> Half a pound
> Burma-Shave. (Verse 101)

Curiously enough, Burma-Shave was one of the very few companies that actually thrived during the Great Depression, a tribute to the product, to the advertising, and to the sense of fun that American people needed during these dark times, and which the signs brought them.

Also in 1934, Burma-Shave began to target certain segments of the shaving population:

> College boys!
> Your courage muster
> Shave off
> That fuzzy
> Cookie duster
> Burma-Shave. (Verse 102)

> Noah had whiskers
> In the ark
> But he wouldn't get by
> On a bench
> In the park
> Burma-Shave. (Verse 103)

was a 1934 jingle that probably wouldn't have been used today, because it targets a segment of the population—Christians, or Bible readers—and would at best not catch the interest of other religious groups, and at worst, alienate them. This jingle also mentions the bench in a park as a place for lovers to spend time, not seen as safe in today's society.

Then, as now, head lice were a problem. This 1936 jingle:

> Cooties love
> Bewhiskered places.
> Cuties love the
> Smoothest faces
> Shaved by
> Burma-Shave. (Verse 104)

What made this ad different from many of Burma-Shave's earlier ones is that their original advertising tack, which had set them apart, had been to get away from the "normal" advertising of the day, scary ads that emphasized negative body aspects, and this was one that hearkened back to the type of advertising that most other companies were producing.

The 1930s was the decade when golf rose to prominence in the United States; in 1934 the Masters Tournament was started at Augusta, Georgia, and several of America's best-known and best-loved golfers began their rise to fame during this decade, Byron Nelson, Ben Hogan, and Sam Snead. Burma-Shave knew a good thing when they saw it, so they began producing golf rhymes, as this one from 1935:

> The happy golfer
> Finds with glee
> The shaves
> That suit him
> To a tee
> Burma-Shave. (Verse 105)

Or,

> Golfers!
> Hole in one
> Is quite a feat
> Unless that hole
> Is in your meat
> Burma-Shave. (Verse 106)

Clinton B. Odell said that his grandfather Clinton M. Odell was a scratch golfer, and his wife Amy was also an excellent golfer.

They also mentioned other sports:

> Fisherman!
> For a lucky strike
> Show the pike
> A face
> They'll like
> Burma-Shave. (Verse 107)

This jingle also shows how more people had to depend on other ways to gather food during the Depression years.

In 1936, proper fashion was dictated by this set of signs:

> Shaving brush
> & soapy smear
> Went out of
> Style with
> Hoops my dear
> Burma-Shave. (Verse 108)

Or perhaps more accurately, what was *not* proper fashion.

Burma-Shave also hearkened to the future, with this 1936 ditty:

> Riot at
> Drug store
> Calling all cars
> 100 customers
> 99 jars
> Burma-Shave. (Verse 83)

which foreshadowed a rollicking police show on television years later.

Burma-Shave was not afraid to throw in the occasional risque rhyme, either:

> Grandpa's beard
> Was stiff and coarse
> And that's what
> Caused his
> Fifth divorce
> Burma-Shave. (Verse 109)

this at a time (1935) when divorce was greatly frowned upon. A later 1935
rhyme read:

> "I just joined,"
> The young man said,
> "A nudist camp.
> Is my face red?
> No! I use
> Burma-Shave." (Verse 110)

In 1936, Burma-Vita produced:

> Jimmie said a
> Naughty word.
> Jimmie's mother overheard.
> Soapsuds? No!
> He preferred
> Burma-Shave. (Verse 111)

during a time when it was seemingly proper and definitely common to wash
a child's mouth out with soap when they said the wrong things, something
that almost never would happen today.

This 1937 jingle:

> Stomachache!
> Doctor—
> Toothache!
> Dentist—
> Whiskers!
> Burma-Shave. (Verse 112)

shows a very different view of health than today, when neither stomach ache
products, or toothache products, are advertised much. But again this ditty is
a window into history during the late 1930s. The lack of electricity to keep
foods frozen led to more food-related and/or stomach problems (the Great
Depression probably also affected people emotionally and stomach-wise), as
well as poorer dental hygiene, fewer dentists, and less of an imperative for
people to visit a dentist—a string tied to the tooth, a slammed door or a
dropped book, and the problem was solved. The precious money that

Americans had was not spent on something so frivolous as dentists, either. Water did not yet routinely contain chemicals to prevent tooth decay, and many Americans got their water from wells.

Burma-Shave signs also introduced new and sometimes radically different concepts, like the 1937 jingle:

> Little Willie
> Modern soul
> Busted papa's
> Brush and bowl.
> Nice work, Willie!
> Burma-Shave. (Verse 113)

Children at the time were used much less in advertisements—a few years earlier the occasional tractor advertisement made mention that the machine was so easy to use that women or children could operate it—but rarely did an advertisement hint that a child should do wrong.

Some of the old Burma-Shave signs also presaged modern lines, like the 1937 one which said:

> Drive
> With care.
> Be alive
> When you
> Arrive.
> Burma-Shave. (Verse 31)

This closely mirrors the "Drive to arrive alive" safety advertising campaign of the latter part of the twentieth century.

A 1935 Burma-Shave sign shows how everyone had a common bond in history, from the Revolutionary past:

> Be a modern
> Paul Revere.
> Spread the news
> From ear
> To ear.
> Burma-Shave. (Verse 114)

Though the name Paul Revere would still probably be recognized by most Americans, there are many others from that era that certainly wouldn't.

Burma-Shave was also not afraid to fracture the English language, an unusual advertising ploy of the times:

> From Saskatoon
> To Alabam',
> You hear men praise
> The shave
> What am
> Burma-Shave. (Verse 115)

Radio shows and literature used slang, idiom, dialect, and other non-standard forms of English—during a time when there was much more of a hoity-toity correctness about the use of the language than there is today—and used these methods successfully. Another one along the same line was this from 1939:

> I proposed
> To Ida.
> Ida refused.
> Ida won my Ida
> If Ida used
> Burma-Shave. (Verse 116)

As America became more mobile, the Burma-Shave ads showed it in subtle ways, as in this 1938 jingle:

> Trail folk
> Have little space
> For totin' things
> To fix the face
> They use
> Burma-Shave. (Verse 117)

Another rhyme that showed some history, and also borrowed a bit of literary erudition, was this 1939 one:

> Hardly a driver
> Is now alive
> Who passed
> On hills
> At 75
> Burma-Shave. (Verse 118)

which hearkened back to another poem, "Paul Revere's Ride," by Henry Wadsworth Longfellow, who wrote in the fourth and fifth lines: "Hardly a man is now alive/Who remembers that famous day and year . . ."

A new type of Burma-Shave signs in 1939 already foreshadowed the end of the company. Better roads, higher speeds (making reading the signs more difficult), and requirements that signs be further from the highways, were beginning to spell doom for the old types of signs. In 1939 Burma-Vita tested some short, or bobtailed, signs, erected near cities where auto speeds were faster. Each of the following lines was a sign set of its own:

A better buy—why not try. Burma-Shave. (Verse 119)
Aid the blade. Burma-Shave. (Verse 120)
A word to the wives is sufficient. Burma-Shave. (Verse 121)
Beard unruly—meet yours truly. Burma-Shave. (Verse 122)
Best reference—public preference. Burma-Shave. (Verse 123)
Better shaving at a saving. Burma-Shave. (Verse 124)
Brush? No! Too slow. Burma-Shave. (Verse 125)
Covers a multitude of chins. Burma-Shave. (Verse 126)
Deluxe de looks with Burma-Shave. (Verse 127)
Don't put it off—put it on. Burma-Shave. (Verse 128)
Economize with this size. Burma-Shave. (Verse 129)
Equip your grip. Burma-Shave. (Verse 130)
50% quicker 100% slicker. Burma-Shave. (Verse 131)
For the faces that go places. Burma-Shave. (Verse 132)
Good to the last strop. Burma-Shave. (Verse 133)
He's nifty and thrifty—looks 30 at 50. Burma-Shave. (Verse 134)
Hot tip, pal—more smiles per gal. Burma-Shave. (Verse 135)

If getting up gets you down—use Burma-Shave. (Verse 136)

Is your face her misfortune? Try Burma-Shave. (Verse 137)

Join the millions using soothing Burma-Shave. (Verse 138)

Just spread, then pat—now shave, that's that! Burma-Shave. (Verse 139)

Look "spiffy" in a "jiffy." Burma-Shave. (Verse 140)

Makes good because it's made good. Burma-Shave. (Verse 141)

Makes misses Mrs. Burma-Shave. (Verse 142)

Nix on nicks. Burma-Shave. (Verse 143)

No digging in on tender skin. Burma-Shave. (Verse 144)

No pushee no pully smooth shavy feel bully. Burma-Shave. (Verse 145)

No sooner spread than done. Burma-Shave. (Verse 146)

No trick to click if quick to pick. Burma-Shave. (Verse 147)

Once a day the easy way. Burma-Shave. (Verse 148)

Other days—other ways. Nowadays Burma-Shave. (Verse 149)

Pays dividends in lady friends. Burma-Shave. (Verse 150)

Right about face. Burma-Shave. (Verse 151)

Romance never starts from scratch. Burma-Shave. (Verse 152)

Saves your jack—holds your Jill. Burma-Shave. (Verse 153)

Shave faster without disaster. Burma-Shave. (Verse 154)

Start the day the modern way. Burma-Shave. (Verse 155)

Takes the "H" out of shave. Burma-Shave. (Verse 156)

Those who click—pick Burma-Shave. (Verse 157)

Try our whisker licker. Burma-Shave. (Verse 158)

When you shop for your pop. Burma-Shave. (Verse 159)

Won by a hair that wasn't there. Burma-Shave. (Verse 160)

You'll enthuse as you use. Burma-Shave. (Verse 161)

Of course, one of the greatest experiences in humankind couldn't be ignored by Burma-Shave, as in this 1948 ditty:

> We don't
> Know how
> To split an atom
> But as to whiskers
> Let us at 'em
> Burma-Shave. (Verse 162)

One of the major events of the century, World War II, also showed up in Burma-Shave ads, this one from 1942:

> Maybe you can't
> Shoulder a gun
> But you can shoulder
> The cost of one
> Buy defense bonds
> Burma-Shave. (Verse 163)

The state of the country's roads was also highlighted in some of the jingles, as this one from 1948, when there were many more curves and the land had not yet been criss-crossed with safer superhighways:

> A man
> A miss
> A car—a curve.
> He kissed the miss
> And missed the curve
> Burma-Shave. (Verse 164)

As inflation rose, Burma-Shave ran special anti-inflation signs:

> Bargain hunters
> Gather round
> For fifty cents
> Still
> Half a pound
> Burma-Shave.
> No price increase. (Verse 165)

Also in 1948,

> Other things have
> Gone sky high
> Half a dollar
> Still will buy
> Half pound jar
> Burma-Shave
> No price increase. (Verse 166)

> With television
> On the set
> Stars are
> Running out
> To get
> Burma-Shave. (Verse 167)

shows America's beginning fascination with television in 1949.

The Pentagon had been built in 1943, but perhaps because Burma-Shave signs were not changed or new ones erected during a four-year span in World War II (gasoline was used only for high wartime priorities, and rubber for tires was almost impossible to get), this rhyme appeared in 1949:

> In seventy years
> Of brushin' soap on
> Gramps coulda painted
> The Pentagon
> Use brushless
> Burma-Shave. (Verse 168)

In 1953, Burma-Shave showed that World War II anger and hatred had all but been eradicated with this sign:

> Gut rasiert? ("If you want a good shave"—German)
> ————Chinese————᠂
> La mejor afeitada ("The best shave"—Spanish)
> The best shave
> In any language
> Burma-Shave. (Verse 169)

Also in 1953, appeared this sign:

> If Crusoe'd kept
> His chin
> More tidy
> He might have found
> A lady Friday,
> Burma-Shave. (Verse 170)

in reference to *The Adventures of Robinson Crusoe,* a movie that came out in 1952.

Few of the later Burma-Shave jingles (1953 to 1963) showed much specific history, partly perhaps because the company was steadily losing market share, and could not afford to target specific parts of the population, which might undermine their efforts to sell Burma-Shave to all members of the population.

One type of jingle which seems conspicuous by its absence is any reference to the Korean Conflict from the early 1950s, but doubtless that omission depended on what jingles the company received. Burma-Vita was not a history company—although their jingles reflected a great deal of it—but a company selling shaving products.

Chapter 18

BURMA-WHAT? OTHER PRODUCTS

*N*ot everybody knows that Burma-Vita company made other products besides Burma-Shave shaving cream. It is well-known that the first product, out of which Burma-Shave developed, was a liniment. But Burma-Vita Company made other products and even erected their telltale trademark six signs by the side of the road for some of them. One of the first of these other products appeared to be Burma-Shave razor blades in 1938:

> Here's the winning
> Shaving team
> The perfect blade
> The perfect cream
> Burma-Shave blade
> Burma-Shave. (Verse 171)

Or,

> Sharpest blade
> Ever made
> Comfort speed
> Guaranteed
> 15 for 25 cents
> Burma-Shave blades
> Burma-Shave. (Verse 172)

Customer Convenience . . .

A WAY TO PROFIT

Yes, Brushless Burma-Shave is packed in tubes and jars for the convenience of shavers, and it gives you an opportunity to increase your sales.

NEW BUYERS EVERY DAY

Younger men go for Burma-Shave in a Big Way because it gives them a clean shaven look that pleases the girl friend.

Cash in on the growing popularity of Burma-Shave. Remember, the new increased Fair Trade Minimum Prices assure greater profits.

Product	Size	Retail	F.T.M.	List per doz.
Burma-Shave	Giant Tube	$ .40	.39	$3.20
Burma-Shave	Medium Jar	.60	.53	4.80
Burma-Shave	Large Jar	1.00	.89	8.00
Burma-Shave Lotion 4-oz bottle		.50	.49	4.00
Burma-Vita Tooth Powder 2¼ oz.		.40	.39	3.20
Burma-Shave Double Edge Razor Blades, pkg. of 15s		.25	.23	2.00

DISCOUNTS From Your Wholesaler:

On all sales representing less than the $3.20 line extension of any product, 2%.

On all sales representing a $3.20 line extension or more of any product excepting as noted below, 5%.

On all sales of original shipping cases or a combination or assortment including at least one original shipping case and other items of not less than $3.20, 7½%.

A March 1949 ad in the *Minnesota Pharmacist.* Note the other products produced by Burma-Vita besides their famous brushless shaving cream.

This is another of the streetcar cards used during the Depression and World War II. It shows the Burma-Shave razor blades as well as the cream.

It seems as though Burma-Shave razor blades were not advertised again—at least on the signs—for another nine years, until 1947:

> You've used
> Our cream
> Now try our blades
> Pair up the best
> In shaving aids
> Burma-Shave. (Verse 173)

Clinton B. Odell said that Burma-Vita bought razor blades from Personna and sold them under its own name.

That same year, Burma-Shave introduced another new product: Burma-Vita Tooth Powder.

> The first
> Improvement
> In many a year
> For cleaning teeth
> Is finally here
> Burma-Vita tooth powder. (Verse 174)

111

The next ones were:

> Speaking of
> Great events
> Burma-Shave
> Proudly presents
> Another fine product
> Burma-Vita tooth powder. (Verse 175)

> Just moisten
> Your tooth brush
> Dip in jar
> And you'll enjoy
> Cleaner teeth by far
> Burma-Vita tooth powder. (Verse 176)

> Better tooth cleanser
> Low expense
> Your druggist
> Sells it
> 40 cents
> Burma-Vita tooth powder. (Verse 177)

Then finally came a few mildly funny ones:

> Don't waste powder
> Down the drain
> By missing brush
> With faulty aim
> A dip does it
> Burma-Vita tooth powder. (Verse 178)

> Tobacco stains
> And stale breath too
> Are two
> Of the things
> It takes from you
> Burma-Vita tooth powder. (Verse 179)

In 1950, Burma-Vita came out with another new product: Burma-Shave Lotion:

> She will
> Flood your face
> With kisses
> 'cause you smell
> So darn delicious
> Burma-Shave lotion. (Verse 180)

Also,

> Use Burma-Shave
> In tube
> Or jar
> Then follow up
> With our new star
> Burma-Shave lotion. (Verse 181)

> It has a tingle
> And a tang
> That starts
> The day off
> With a bang
> Burma-Shave lotion. (Verse 182)

> Bracing as
> An ocean breeze
> For after shaving
> It's sure
> To please
> Burma-Shave lotion. (Verse 183)

> For early
> Morning
> Pep and bounce
> A brand new product
> We announce
> Burma-Shave lotion. (Verse 184)

The ladies
Take one whiff
And purr
It's no wonder
Men prefer
Burma-Shave lotion. (Verse 185)

They also used an old Burma-Shave standby rhyme, and simply added "lotion" to it:

His face
Was smooth
And cool as ice
And oh! Louise!
He smelled so nice
Burma-Shave lotion.

This one had originally come out in 1935, advertising just Burma-Shave.

In magazines, Burma-Shave lotion was advertised this way: "If you haven't purchased a bottle of Burma-Shave Lotion, and sent us the carton, there is still time for you to take advantage of this outstanding offer. We are willing and anxious to buy you your first bottle of Burma-Shave Lotion. We will pay the 50¢ purchase price plus the tax if you will mail us the carton with your name and address . . ." This offer was made at the University of Minnesota only.

Burma-Vita also plugged its lotion by taking testimonials from University of Minnesota people: From A.L.P. "Its refreshing odor is something out of the ordinary. It's most outstanding feature is its mild action on skin tenderized by shaving."

From P.C. "I am going to be one of its steady customers. It leaves my face cool and smooth—A typical Burma-Vita product—perfectly satisfactory."

And From R. L.: "It has a definite masculine aroma that appeals to the most demanding of females."

One of the products that Burma-Vita produced that was not in its Burma-Shave line was a mosquito cream: "We manufacture B-V Mosquito

Cream (discovered in a swamp). June, July, and August are the months to sell it," the advertising said. It is unclear if there were ever any signs by the side of the road promoting the mosquito cream, but probably not.

Steve Soelberg, a major collector of Burma-Shave items, said the mosquito repellent was not produced commercially. "It was a test run that didn't go over."

Soelberg added that Burma-Vita also produced a pre-shave electric lo-

NOW IS THE TIME TO SELL MOSQUITO CREAM

We manufacture B-V Mosquito Cream (discovered in a swamp). June, July, and August are the months to sell it.

Price $48.00 per gross, less 16⅔% and 2%, freight paid.

We pay 25c per dozen special commission to your salesmen for sales of B-V Mosquito Cream.

Free goods to trade same as Burma-Shave.

tion, and a talcum powder. Clinton B. Odell said, "At the end of their existence they produced an after shave called Burma Bey, a deodorant called Burma-Blockade, in an aerosol bomb." He added that the shaving cream was being produced in jars and in tubes, as well.

None of the rhymes or ditties written to promote these other products had much impact, or are memorable. Perhaps it is simply because the bright light of success so fell on Burma-Shave signs that all others were always in shadow by comparison, or perhaps it was simply that adding one word at the end of Burma-Shave, i.e., "lotion," upset some delicate kind of balance in the rhyme; or maybe it was simply that the jingles that were written for these other products were written to describe the product—which

Burma-Shave seldom did—and were actually to "straight-advertise" the products. In other words, perhaps these products didn't start first in a spirit of fun—perhaps it was impossible to make Mosquito Cream funny, for instance—but at any rate, the signs for these products simply didn't work nearly as well as the ones for Burma-Shave did.

Burma-Shave was best-known in a jar, then in a tube, but it also came out in a giant yellow can called, "the Bomb."

Chapter 19

"MODERN" BURMA-SHAVE SIGNS

*I*f it is true that imitation is the sincerest form of flattery, then Burma-Shave has been flattered indeed throughout the years. The Burma-Shave signs, or the Burma-Shave concept, have been used in countless different ways since the company actually went out of business, and the signs were taken down.

Burma-Shave signs have been used and abused on all kinds of media, as well. Years ago *Mad Magazine* parodied Burma-Shave thus:

Her guy's whiskers
Just don't faze her
He shaves by
Electric razor
Why bother with
Burma Shave?

Though the founders of the company probably wouldn't have been too endeared to this rhyme, they would have to give credence to the idea that the Burma-Shave concept that they started and nurtured is still well and alive.

Burma-Shave has even been used on-stage recently. Peter Vaughan critiqued a recent Minneapolis play, "On the Verge," saying, "I lost track of how many times Burma-Shave and Ike were mentioned as the girdled, umbrella-wielding ladies encountered a rock 'n' roll star, a biker, a lounge lizard and a prototypical adenoidal teenager, all played with panache by Dale Pfeilsticker."

Though this is probably not how many people would like to have Burma-Shave remembered, this shows that it *is* remembered.

An article published on July 11, 1997, in the *Pioneer Press* newspaper said of the 1997 United States Martian space adventure, "The only reason to watch that little robot bump over the surface of Mars is to see if it stumbles across a rusty Chevy up on jacks or a series of faded Burma-Shave signs or a pile of cigarette butts, anything to provide evidence of life as we know it."

Morgan Richardson wrote that, "Years ago on a Jack Benny radio drama, Dennis Day was lost and crawling through a dense jungle. He was startled to see a series of signs that he read out loud:

> Ugga-wugga
> Ogga-lave
> Igga-wigga
> Burma-Shave.

Modern Burma-Shave signs have been erected to try to slow traffic down. For instance, Albuquerque, New Mexico, has made use of Burma-Shave signs, cautioning drivers to slow down through a four-mile construction zone. *Business Week* said in their December 30, 1996, issue that "The fun is the gradual unfolding of a rhyme as the signs zip by. Four signs, about one-tenth of a mile apart, encourage the 130,000 motorists who drive daily along Interstate 40 to obey the forty-five mph speed limit. That's ten mph slower than the usual allowable speed. The agency got the jingle from a contest a radio station ran. The message:

> Through this maze of machines and rubble
> Driving fast can cause you trouble
> Take care and be alert
> So no one on this road gets hurt."

Some have used the Burma-Shave sign concept to combine speed and environment protection. This should not surprise anyone, since the original brain trust of Burma-Vita held lowering speeds in high esteem, and many of their jingles are directed that way.

In California, hand-written Burma-Shave signs have been posted along Beverly Glen Road north of Sunset Boulevard, recounting the killings of a deer buck and an owl by speeding drivers. The signs plead for sanity on the roads, and the last line rhymes with the speed limit (thirty-five miles per hour), and said, "Keep them alive."

On Delphi.com, Dan Culbertson reported that another set of signs near where he lives said:

> Down the hill
> Lickety split
> It's a beautiful deer
> Wasn't it?

This is a play on an original 1953 Burma-Shave sign ("Around the curve, lickety-split, it's a beautiful car, wasn't it? Burma-Shave." Verse 81)

Also, Burma-Shave signs have been recently used in Oklahoma to get people to pay closer attention to the environment after a small grass fire burned over a short section of right-of-way beside a rural Oklahoma road. When the long dead grass had been burned up by the fire, a startling sight was seen: nearly 300 bottles and cans were revealed along only a 200-yard swath of highway, one discarded container for every two feet of road frontage, "a statistic," *Blair & Ketchum's Country Journal* wrote, "that won't surprise many Oklahoma farmers. They know from sad experience that their state has a serious litter problem."

To combat the problem, the Oklahoma Farm Bureau reverted to the old Burma-Shave sign concept. "Now farmers throughout Oklahoma are putting similar sets of signs along their roadside fences, with slogans like the following:

> Come on, Okies
> Take a stand
> Let's clean up
> This littered
> Land
> Farm Bureau.

And:

> I raise cows
> They eat hay
> Don't throw
> Trash on
> The right of way.
> Farm Bureau.

Farmers pay fifty dollars for a set of six signs, with six different choices of verses, and then set them up on their own land as close to the roadside as possible but inside the fenceline. "The signs are spaced thirty yards apart," *Country Journal* wrote, "so a motorist traveling at the speed limit will have a couple of seconds to read each one." Peeler said the signs seemed to be working. "Many members say they've noticed a reduction in the amount of litter thrown on their fields since they put the signs up."

Other signs add a penalty: $100 reward for information leading to the conviction of anyone littering a member's property, *Country Journal* reported.

Nor should anyone have been surprised that the concept would be used in a backwards way, to try to convince government officials to *increase* speeds:

Patrick Bedard wrote in *Car and Driver* magazine about cancelling the fifty-five-mile-per-hour speed limit, and he used Burma-Shave to promote it: "Besides," he wrote, "I think this particular ad campaign will appeal to Reagan's show-biz sense.

"Generally, they fell into four categories, the first emphasizing the fate awaiting the incautious:

> Spring
> Has sprung
> The grass has riz
> Where last year's
> Careless driver is.
> Burma-Shave. (Verse 186)

"Speeding, then as now, was a popular target for safety sloganeers. Drinking drivers were given their share of attention, too.

"The most potent of all highway distractions has pretty much been neutralized by the advent of the bucket seat, but Burma-Shave didn't wait. It did what it could with what it had:

> If hugging
> On highways
> Is your sport
> Trade in your car
> For a davenport.
> Burma-Shave. (Verse 37)

"You can always tell, by the way the paternalistic poohbahs in Washington go about their business, that the federal government has never meant to be a profit maker. If it was, it would soon learn that ideas can't be forced down people's throats. Burma-Shave shrewdly couched its messages in terms the public would even stop and back up to read. If the government really wants to save lives—and not just be the boss—it should adopt a similar method. And just to kick off the program, I'll throw in a free verse, fresh baked for the eighties:

> As to belts
> He was
> No taker
> Had a crash
> And met his maker."

The Burma-Shave concept has been used in classrooms, where teachers have contests for kids making Burma-Shave-like signs as writing exercises; magazines have used the concept in contests, as when *Atlantic Monthly* magazine held an on-line contest called "Jingle All the Way," started by Emily Cox and Henry Rathvon, the creators of the Atlantic Puzzler. Some that Guy Jacobson found at Christmas 1996 by the side of the road, included:

Take a turn
Behind the wheel
It's not
Your father's
Oldsmobile.

Is your coach
A little dry?
When you win
Anoint the guy.
Gatorade.

Crystal waters,
Blue and clear.
Caribbean?
No, my dear.
Tidy Bowl.

Two that Cox and Rathvon penned as examples:

Remember what
The barkeep said,
With Sudsman beer,
You get a head.

Sam and Dave
And Nat King Cole
Had lots
Of heart
But we have sole.
Fleischman's fish.

The three winners of the contest were given a free book courtesy of *Atlantic Monthly*. The envelopes, please . . . but first:

Your game hosts thank
Each male and female
Who filled our box
With punning e-mail.
Cox and Rathvon.

122

"But to get the proper effect of that jingle," they wrote, "—and the ones below from our contest, you probably should put each line on its own placard and space them at the side of a highway somewhere, and then drive past them at about sixty miles per hour . . ."

> Skip the puzzles
> Quit the yak
> We just want
> Those red
> Signs back.
> The Pin Family.

The winners:

> Balding early?
> Don't despair
> Something new
> Is in the hair.
> Rogaine. (By Mary@surfsouth.com)

> Aitch tee tee pee
> Colon slash slash
> You really can
> Make.quick.cash.
> WEBSCAMS.COM. (By LeonardJK)

> Sir Galahad
> Took a bite.
> It locked
> His jaw.
> Silent night.
> Betty Botter Better Peanut Butter.
> (By Birdsinger)

Other favorites included:

> Save our forests
> From abuse;
> Buy a
> Polyester spruce.
> Ersatz Trees, Inc. (By ShedPot)

The sun seems bright
The stars aligned.
All Ken's troubles
Are left behind.
PREPARATION H. (By nickp@ormutual.com)

Have some drinks
Crash some cars
Spend some time
Behind our bars.
HIGHWAY PATROL. (LeonardJK)

Chris and Mary
Lived at Pa's,
But at Yuletide
Mary, Chris—Ma's.
Share the Kids Support Group. (By Birdsinger)

There were many more at this site, which shows how alive the concept of Burma-Shave signs still is today.

Other Burma-Shave contests are less genteel, as the Richard Nixon Memorial Burma-Shave Showdown, another on-line contest basically to make fun of Richard Nixon:

Nixon got us
In with China
Now he's
Gone to
Something fina.
Burma Shave.

Along with the winner of the contest, by Scott Dorsey:

Dickie slept
Through Martin's dream.
At least he kept
His tape heads clean
With Burma Shave.

Second place went to Ilana, for:

> Now he's six feet
> Underground
> Won't have Dick to
> Kick around.
> Burma Shave.

Other entries in this contest included:

> You can cross the
> Mason-Dixon
> But you
> Can't cross
> Richard Nixon
> Burma Shave.

> On droopy jowls
> 'Neath ski slope nose,
> Tricky Dick's five o'clock
> Shadow grows.
> Burma Shave.

John Lowery wrote about a Burma-Shave sign that was never a Burma-Shave sign: "I must have been about ten years old (sixty-five years ago) when I thought this one up. Never did send it in [to the contests] in spite of many urgings:

> The bearded lady
> Took a chance
> Now she's queen
> Of the fairy dance.
> Burma-Shave.

James Bockhaus of Morton, Illinois, said he wrote a series of Burma-Shave-like signs for his daughter's high school marching band. "There's a fair amount of high school band competition in the Midwest, so every Saturday the marching band of our local high school goes to another area where a number of other marching bands have been invited as well, and they have what they call a field competition."

125

Morton High School band parents of Morton, Illinois, exhibit a modern way to use Burma-Shave-like signs: to urge their high school marching band on during competitions.

Parents in their loosely-organized band club always tried to do something special for the band for every competition, and Bockhaus came up with the idea of making Burma-Shave-like signs. "I took lucite and painted one side black and red, the marching band's colors, and on the other side I used white shoe polish to put a slogan on."

Those slogans were rhymes that often featured the names of other towns against whom the competition was being held:

> Show that pride
> Stand up tall
> At Pekin parade
> We'll take it all
> Morton High School
> Marching Band

> With pride and pizzazz
> To Western we go
> Reach for the sky
> And steal the show.
> Morton High School
> Marching Band

We love you Morton
Seniors you're great
Go out and show 'em
You're best in the state.
Morton High School
Marching Band

They always knew the route the band was going to take, so they went out there in advance with the signs, and stood at a safe spot off the road, and held up the signs for the students to read. "The band parents group which held the signs had a good time, and the band came to expect the weekly 'surprise,'" Bockhaus said.

Burma-Shave was revived in the 1996 United States presidential election, as John McCaslin wrote in the *Washington Times* on September 1, 1996, when he told of the Virginia Young Republicans reviving the decades-old tradition of signs by the side of the road along Key Bridge, which connects Virginia and Washington, D.C., over the Potomac River. "But they weren't hawking shaving cream," McCaslin wrote. "The four signs read:

If you're tired of a White House
That's always smokin' hemp
Vote for our future
Vote Dole-Kemp!

McCaslin added that the signs were the brainchild of Young Republicans member James Parmalee, who said he thought up the rhyme at a meeting of the group on August 13. "Some morning commuters honked in support, he said," McCaslin wrote, "while others gave the political verse a thumbs-down." Parmalee added that he doubted that today's young people knew about Burma-Vita's advertising campaign using doggerel verse in a series of signs set up alongside the highways of the country, but he also figured his own message didn't go over anyone's head. "We figure they don't know what Burma-Shave is," he said, "but they know what hemp is." He added that the campaign might see more Burma-Shave-type signs as he thought of rhymes for Dole, Bob, and Jack.

It is possible to bring back the Burma-Shave signs, but not the times that made them work. (Courtesy of the Stearns County Historical Society, St. Cloud, Minnesota)

The revival of Burma-Shave signs, and then Burma-Shave as a product, has elicited many strong opinions, as in a 1997 *Newsday* article:

> American Drivers
> Once traveled miles
> Past catchy signs
> That brought them smiles.
> Burma-Shave.

The article tells about American Safety Razor company's comeback with Burma-Shave, using thirty-second television commercials. Signs were to be erected in a dozen states, and several baseball parks.

Then, Lewis Lord wrote in *U.S. News & World Report* that "The thirty-second spot opens with a smooth-shaven man in his mid-fifties driving down a seaside road, a younger woman at his side. Although the couple ride in a fiery 1958 Chevrolet Corvette, the little red signs they pass have a touchy-feely refrain fresh from the '90s: You don't have a care, you don't have a worry, you've reached the point, where you don't have to hurry, Burma-Shave. At the final sign, a question appears on the TV screen: 'Where will it take you?' Since the Corvette is last seen empty and parked beside the beach, the not-too-subtle answer seems to be that Burma-Shave takes this shaver and his squeeze to an unhurried moment behind the dunes."

Lord said the new ads miss entirely the concept that Burma-Shave was meant to give, and what is shown in Rowsome's book, *The Verse by the Side of the Road,* calling the essential spirit of Burma-Shave "the lighthearted humor of its jaunty doggerel."

Lord added that no one in a real Burma-Shave rhyme rolled in the sand, "though many a woolly Lothario struck out trying. Like in this jingle:

> He played
> A sax
> Had no B.O.
> But his whiskers scratched
> So she let him go,
> Burma-Shave. (Verse 16)

"Sometimes the rejections were quite vivid:

> To get
> Away from
> Hairy Apes,
> Ladies jump
> From fire escapes.
> Burma-Shave. (Verse 87)

"The advice to the hirsute never let up:

> Dinah doesn't
> Treat him right
> But if he'd
> Shave
> Dyna-mite!
> Burma-Shave. (Verse 187)

"Some verses were Shakespearean:

> Said Juliet
> To Romeo
> "If you
> Won't shave
> Go homeo"
> Burma-Shave." (Verse 188)

Lord continued by saying that only a shrinking minority of today's American population ever enjoyed the real Burma-Shave rhymes, and that to keep the campaign authentically nostalgic, American Safety Razor Company "might try a few ads displaying authentic Burma-Shave rhymes. . . . Instead of a sterile assertion that there is nothing to fret about, the aging boomers could be given a potent proverb from 1943: 'Within this vale of toil and sin, your head grows bald but not your chin. Burma-Shave.' That's truth in advertising."

We Americans listed one "real" Burma-Shave sign (His tenor voice she thought divine till whiskers scratched sweet Adeline, Burma-Shave. Verse 463), and then these:

> Twenties tourists
> Washed their hair
> Neath trees 'n tarp
> And open air.
> Ramblers rave.

And,

> The bright red signs
> We used to see 'em
> But now they're gone
> To the museum
> Jingles brave.

> From '25
> To '63
> We rode and read
> Then came TV
> O changing wave.

And finally,

> Now ads on tubes
> Are signs of times
> But how we miss
> Those funny rhymes
> O Burma-Shave.

Burma-Shave signs have even recently been used in a "Burma-Slave" campaign, as part of the effort to build the boycott against companies supporting the Burmese dictators. Examples:

> Burmese children
> Build the roads
> To bring you gas
> To help you go
> Slave labor is the hidden cost
> When you pull into
> [Company]
> Burma-Shave.

> Our money goes
> To enslave the masses.
> Set Burma free
> Boycott [company] gases.
> Burma-Shave.

Burma-Shave signs and the concept appear in all kinds of other places, as well: Dr. J. Robert Lundy launched California's Route 66 revival in 1989, resulting in the Rancho Cucamonga Visitors Center, where visitors can see exhibits, paintings, automotive parts, tools, and equipment showing the history of that famous highway between Los Angeles and Chicago. "Check out the Burma-Shave signs as you listen to sixteen different renditions of 'Route 66' playing in the background.'"

Reminisce magazine also has started a Burma-Shave-type sign promotion advertising its magazine; erecting signs in more than forty states. The signs are the same color as the old Burma-Shave signs, with the similar messages, but the last line said Reminisce.

In a most unusual twist on the Burma-Shave signs, the *Pioneer Press* of St. Paul wrote April 15, 1994, that the Doggerel Committee turned to Burma-Shave-like verse to give them the scoop on picking up dog poop instead of letting it lie on other people's and public lawns, and streets and sidewalks.

Also in Minnesota, rhyming signs along Itasca County trails bring smiles to the faces of snowmobilers, the *Pioneer Press* reported in 1993.

On Interstate 45 at the Holzwarth Road exit near Spring, Texas, in 1991, The Art Guys operated a roadside stand selling birdhouses made of many different materials. To get people's attention, they spaced teaser signs along the highway: "These signs are not for laughs alone. Buy a birdhouse or go back home."

The Burma-Shave concept was even used as a foreword in a book, which had nothing to do with Burma-Shave, by the grandson of the founders of the company, George Hamley Odell. "I'm an archaeologist, essentially an academic who wrote books for a living. I wrote about a project we had in the Illinois Valley of Illinois, and called the book *Stone Tools and Mobility in the Illinois Valley*. It came out in 1996 by the International Monographs and Prehistory Press in Ann Arbor, Michigan. That book is dedicated to my parents, and it has a set of signs with a fictive jingle on it."

Some people claim that even towards the end of the Twentieth Century there are still Burma-Shave signs posted in hidden outbacks across America; doubtless this is wishful thinking, since renting farmers' land for the signs cost money, and since Philip Morris Company took all the signs down in the mid-sixties.

That, of course, has not stopped people from devising their own modern Burma-Shave signs and uses. Burma-Shave products can be ordered on the internet, and the ways the signs have been used are as many as there are creative ideas.

But in the reincarnation of Burma-Shave signs, nobody came close to reproducing the excitement and fun of the original ones.

When Burma-Shave sign creator Allan G. Odell died, *USA Today* wrote:

Don't look now
But if you must,
An ad man's gem
Has bit
The dust. . .
Burma-Shave.

Chapter 20

SO WHAT HAPPENED?

*I*f the small company from Minnesota could increase its gross from zero in 1926 to more than three million dollars during its heyday, why did the company and Burma-Shave go out of business in the early 1960s?

William Childress wrote in an article in *Geico Direct* in 1991: "Until about 1955 the little white-on-red road signs made their products all time best-sellers. Then, thirty years after the Odells hand-painted some letters on planks from a lumber yard, something happened. The brothers never satisfactorily found out what, but theories abounded, some of them plausible."

Just as several reasons propelled Burma-Shave to the forefront, so a number of reasons toppled it:

First, the highways.

MUSA on-line: "But eventually times changed. America's countryside shrank due to superhighways and faster cars. Huge billboards outshouted the little signs."

"We even tried large billboard signs," Grace said, "but they didn't work." Highways were better, wider, and cars went faster, so it was impossible to read the Burma-Shave signs as people once had. In a sense, people forgot about them.

Second, the cost of maintaining the signs. From its first humble beginnings, when Allan Odell had to sell forty-nine percent of the company, Burma-Shave grew steadily. It took in $68,000 the first year after the signs had been implanted along the roads, and the first repeat orders ever came from druggists in those Minnesota areas where the signs had been. The company also spent that year (1926) $25,000 for advertising, as signs were installed in the rest of Minnesota, Iowa, and Wisconsin. Sales doubled in 1927, and sign expenditures were $45,000 and were by then in most states in the Midwest. "By 1929," wrote Evelyn S. Dorman in *The Encyclopedia of Consumer Brands*, "Burma-Vita was spending approximately $65,000 in ads, with sales averaging around a quarter of a million. The company began grossing more than three million dollars a year as signs could be found from coast to coast."

The signs had always been expensive to maintain, because they were constantly in danger of degrading in weather and by animals. Plus, there was great cost in sending trucks all over the United States to check on the signs, and replace those that needed replacing, or changing old ones to new ones. The signs had simply become too labor intensive and expensive.

Third, America's move toward urbanism, which changed how people thought and acted. The little poems were rural oriented, and America was becoming more and more urban.

Signs like

> You know
> Your onions
> Lettuce suppose
> This beets them all
> Don't turnip your nose
> Burma-Shave. (Verse 189)

just didn't work or make sense to urbanites who had no garden or time for one.

Fourth, fewer farmers. Farmers had always been Burma-Shave's staunchest allies; but with the family farm all but disappearing, huge conglomerates were not interested in advertising for Burma-Shave, and the minimal income the signs brought in didn't interest them.

Fifth, the old ways changed. Where once people had flocked to Burma-Shave as a product because the company represented clean and wholesome all-American values, that no longer seemed to matter to many people, and so the wholesome-oriented signs just weren't as palatable as they had been. The times had simply changed; it was like trying to sell polyester

135

leisure suits in the 1990s. It could probably be done, but it wouldn't be easy.

Sixth, competition. There were also a great many shaving competitors in the marketplace, and Burma-Shave simply could not hold its share, nor remain profitable.

Seventh, branching out. Though the officials at Burma-Vita might disagree, the fact that they started trying to market other products probably had an effect. Many other companies have regretted moving away from the products that they made best, using time, people, and resources on the new product, only to find that when they turn back, they find that they have not only not done well with the new products—like Burma-Shave lotion, and talcum powder and razor blades, for example—but that their main product has also started to slip.

Eighth, the jingles. Where they had been lighthearted and whimsical and fun, in the later years, the jingles started to bog down, especially in the mid to late 1950s. They simply weren't as much fun as they had been (to which Clinton B. Odell wholeheartedly disagreed: "They were always fun," he said).

Signs were not changed as often, and people got bored with the same signs on their routes. Most people who talk about the rhymes talk about the early ones:

> Pity all
> The mighty Caesars.
> They pulled
> Each whisker out
> With tweezers.
> Burma-Shave. (Verse 190)

As opposed to later ones:

> The band
> For which
> The grandstand roots
> Is not made up
> Of substi-toots.
> Burma-Shave. (Verse 191)

The earlier rhymes seem more fun and powerful than many of the later ones.

Ninth, their time had passed. The signs and rhymes were no longer different and unique. Burma-Shave had come into existence at exactly the right time, when everything converged to make its existence favorable; by the late 1950s, all of those forces had changed. Allan Odell told William Zinsser in a *Saturday Evening Post* article, "I don't know if I'd get the same response if I started putting up those signs today. Some of the fire and vigor have gone out." The company apparently believed this was true, as they began rerunning old jingles from the 1930s on signs in the early sixties.

As Dorman wrote in *The Encyclopedia of Brand Names*, "All good things come to an end, and the end for Burma-Vita Company was evident in 1948, when sales declined and costs increased, prompting salary cuts. Eventually the jingles just wore out and were temporarily abandoned in favor of television and radio advertising. People were also beginning to drive too fast to read the signs. The old time highways of yore were turning into high-speed expressways. Signs were becoming costlier and less effective, and complaints about billboard pollution mounted."

Whatever happened, by 1963 the Odells had come to the conclusion that Burma-Shave was no longer working; they sold the company to Phillip Morris. George Hamley Odell said, "After they decided to sell the company, I had the sense of a great opportunity being lost. It came as a surprise to me that it was being sold. But it was losing market share. It wasn't selling as much as Barbasol or its other competitors, and I think they probably got out of it at the right time."

Farmers were told that they could keep the signs, and many took them down and saved them. Some collectors stole signs; others went around and bought them.

"By 1978," wrote Dorman in *The Encyclopedia of Consumer Brands*, "Philip Morris discontinued all rights to such Burma-Vita trademarks as Burma-Shave, Burma Bey, Burma Blockade, and Burma Face-Guard, reported John J. O'Connor in *Advertising Age*."

By this time, Burma products had not been marketed for nearly a year. Philip Morris sold the Burma trademarks to American Safety Razor Products, then a division of Philip Morris.

By the early 1960s, the decision was made to discontinue Burma-Shave. "Crews in trucks," Dunlops wrote, "fanned across the country to unbolt signs and uproot posts, so that nothing remained of what had been. Farmers often seemed sad at the removal, not so much at the loss of income, but because, 'It's sort of like losing an old friend.'"

Joe Blackstock, said, "Think of Burma-Shave as being a unique and distinctive form of outdoor advertising. None of the big companies ever connected with those kinds of signs. Burma-Shave was a completely distinctive and unique form of outdoor advertising. There had never been anything like it before, and there hasn't been anything like it since. It had no effect on outdoor advertising in general, except that outdoor people like myself always referred to it in a good way, because it showed that putting roadside messages out there is a good idea, whether the signs are big or small.

"The discontinuation of Burma-Shave jingles met with public farewells conducted in the mainstream press. The Advertising Club of New York held a luncheon to bid adieu and introduce a Eurasian actress who would become the Burma-Shave TV spokeperson. Some of the signs were given to the Smithsonian Institute for posterity. In all, some 35,000 individual Burma-Shave signs had dotted the United States' highways and byways. (Other figures say 700 different jingles on 40,000 signs.)

"Advertising trade journals claimed that the Odells had 'set off a wave of nostalgia' and that the 'signs were having as many retirements as an aging opera star.'"

What was it about the verses that tickled America's funny bone? According to George Odell, Allan's son, who wrote a graduate school dissertation on the Burma-Vita Company, the jingles had a typically Western humor of exaggeration: "We've made grandpa look so trim the local draft board's after him. Burma-Shave." Other writers such as Mark Twain had employed the same brand of humor, he said.

"George felt that, to travelers, 'It was reassuring to find a chatty, familiar jingle on a roadway miles from home. Almost inevitably the impression was given that the company sure must be made up of friendly plain folks, very different from those other advertisers of drug-store products, who noisily threatened malodorousness, disease, and decay."

Whatever conspired to take Burma-Shave from the lives of people who loved the signs, they are gone. People could jaw about their loss all they wanted, but in the end, they have to face it. It was one more indignity from modern life they had to take on the chin.

Chapter 21

THE REMAINING BURMA-SHAVE RHYMES
NOT USED ELSEWHERE

Lather was used
By Daniel Boone
He lived
A 100 years
Too soon
Burma-Shave. (Verse 192)

Eeny-meeny
Miny-mo
Save your skin
Your time
Your dough
Burma-Shave. (Verse 193)

Water heater
Out of kilter
Try the brushless
Whisker
Wilter
Burma-Shave. (Verse 194)

Half a pound
For
Half a dollar
Spread on thin
Above the collar
Burma-Shave. (Verse 195)

Shaving brushes
Such a bother
Burma-Shave
Looks good
To
Father. (Verse 196)

Be
No
Longer
Lather's slave
Treat yourself to
Burma-Shave. (Verse 197)

Tho stiff
The beard
That Nature gave
It shaves like down
With
Burma-Shave. (Verse 198)

Here's
A good deed
For a scout
Tell your dad
All about
Burma-Shave. (Verse 199)

She kissed
The hairbrush
By mistake
She thought it was
Her husband Jake
Burma-Shave. (Verse 200)

When better
Shaving brushes
Are made
We'll still shave
Without their aid
Burma-Shave. (Verse 201)

If every sip
Fills you
With zip
Then your sipper
Needs a zipper
Burma-Shave. (Verse 202)

Iceman's grandson
Now full grown
Has cooling system
All his own
He uses
Burma-Shave. (Verse 203)

Twinkle, twinkle
One-eyed car
We all wonder
WHERE
You are
Burma-Shave. (Verse 204)

A whiskery kiss
For the one
You adore
May not make her mad
But her face will be sore
Burma-Shave. (Verse 205)

Doesn't
Kiss you
Like she useter?
Perhaps she's seen
A smoother rooster
Burma-Shave. (Verse 206)

Train wrecks few
Reason clear
Fireman
Never hugs
Engineer
Burma-Shave. (Verse 207)

Toughest
Whiskers
In the town
We hold 'em up
You mow em down
Burma-Shave. (Verse 208)

The hero
Was brave and strong
And willin'
She felt his chin—
Then wed the villain
Burma-Shave. (Verse 209)

One shave lasts
All day through
Face feels
Cool and
Smoother too
Burma-Shave. (Verse 210)

Grandpa knows
It ain't too late
He's gone
To git
Some widder bait
Burma-Shave. (Verse 211)

6 million housewives
Can't be wrong
Who keep
Their husbands
Right along in
Burma-Shave. (Verse 212)

The draftee
Tried a tube
And purred
Well whaddya know
I've been defurred
Burma-Shave. (Verse 213)

Don't
Try passing
On a slope
Unless you have
A periscope
Burma-Shave. (Verse 214)

The poorest guy
In the
Human race
Can have a
Million dollar face
Burma-Shave. (Verse 215)

Tempted to try it?
Follow your hunch
Be "Top Banana"
Not one
Of the bunch
Burma-Shave. (Verse 216)

Henry the Eighth
Sure had
Trouble
Short-term wives
Long-term stubble
Burma-Shave. (Verse 217)

Thirty days
Hath September
April
June and the
Speed offender
Burma-Shave. (Verse 218)

Statistics prove
Near and far
That folks who
Drive like crazy
—Are
Burma-Shave. (Verse 219)

If our road signs
Catch your eye
Smile
But don't forget
To buy
Burma-Shave. (Verse 220)

Five
Hundred
Thousand
Men
Use
Burma-Shave. (Verse 221)

It's a good
Old Spanish custom
Take your mug
And brush
And bust 'em
Burma-Shave. (Verse 222)

Late Risers
Shave in just
2 minutes flat
Kiss your wife
Grab your hat
Burma-Shave. (Verse 223)

To shaving brush
I need
Not cling
I will not hush
Of thee I sing
Burma-Shave. (Verse 224)

Buy a tube
Use it one week
If you then want
Your money back
Send us the tube
Burma-Shave. (Verse 225)

Bridge prize
For men
Just half a buck
Try it, hostess
Change your luck
Burma-Shave. (Verse 226)

Listen shavers
Knock on wood
When offered
Something
"Just as good"
Burma-Shave. (Verse 227)

Your beauty, boys
Is just
Skin deep
What skin you've got
You ought to keep
Burma-Shave. (Verse 228)

Modern man
Spreads it on
Pats it in
Shaves it off
See him grin
Burma-Shave. (Verse 229)

From New York town
To Pumpkin Holler
It's half a pound
For
Half a dollar
Burma-Shave. (Verse 230)

Put your brush
Back on the shelf
The darn thing
Needs a
Shave itself
Burma-Shave. (Verse 231)

Ashes to ashes
Forests to dust
Keep Minnesota green
Or we'll
All go bust
Burma-Shave. (Verse 232)

Here's something
That could
Even soak
The whiskers off
A radio joke
Burma-Shave. (Verse 233)

Little Bo-Peep
Has lost her Jeep
It struck
A truck
When she went to sleep
Burma-Shave. (Verse 234)

Angels
Who guard you
When you drive
Usually
Retire at 65
Burma-Shave. (Verse 235)

Tested
In peace
Proven in war
Better now
Than ever before
Burma-Shave. (Verse 236)

Speed
Was high
Weather was not
Tires were thin
X marks the spot
Burma-Shave. (Verse 237)

Dim your lights
Behind a car
Let folks see
How bright
YOU are
Burma-Shave. (Verse 238)

Ben
Met Anna
Made a hit
Neglected beard
Ben-Anna split
Burma-Shave. (Verse 239)

The game laws
Ought to
Let you shoot
The bird who hands you
A substitute
Burma-Shave. (Verse 240)

All these years
Your skin
Has dried
Why not moisten
Up your hide
Burma-Shave. (Verse 241)

The answer to
A shaver's dream
A greaseless
No brush
Shaving cream
Burma-Shave. (Verse 242)

Kids! Attention!
44 best jingles
Used so far
In jingle book
With tube or jar
Burma-Shave. (Verse 243)

As you Journey
Down the years
Your mirror is
The glass that cheers
If you use
Burma-Shave. (Verse 244)

The hobo
Lets his
Whiskers sprout
It's trains—not girls
That he takes out
Burma-Shave. (Verse 245)

Bristly beard
Or silky fuzz
Just shave 'em back
To where
They was
Burma-Shave. (Verse 246)

If you have
A double chin
You've two
Good reasons
To begin using
Burma-Shave. (Verse 247)

Romances are wrecked
Before they begin
By a hair
On the coat
Or a lot on the chin
Burma-Shave. (Verse 248)

Say, big boy
To go
Thru life
How'd you like
A whiskered wife?
Burma-Shave. (Verse 249)

Henry the Eighth
Prince of friskers
Lost five wives
But kept
His whiskers
Burma-Shave. (Verse 250)

Let's give the
Clerk a hand
Who never
Palms off
Another brand
Burma-Shave. (Verse 251)

To every man
His shave
Is best
Until he makes
The final test
Burma-Shave. (Verse 252)

Pedro
Walked
Back home by golly
His bristly chin
Was hot-to-Molly
Burma-Shave. (Verse 253)

Train approaching
Whistle squealing
Pause!
Avoid that
Rundown feeling!
Burma-Shave. (Verse 254)

Helps
Your budget
Hold its ground
Half a dollar
Half a pound
Burma-Shave. (Verse 255)

Cutie invited
Varsity hop
Guy full
Of whiskers
Party a flop
Burma-Shave. (Verse 256)

Join
Our happy
Brushless throng
Six million users
Can't be wrong
Burma-Shave. (Verse 257)

Why work up
A daily lather
Once you've tried
We're sure
You'd rather
Burma-Shave. (Verse 258)

Shaving brush
Is out of date
Use the
Razor's
Perfect mate
Burma-Shave. (Verse 259)

Broken romance
Stated fully
She went wild
When he
Went wooly
Burma-Shave. (Verse 260)

A whiskered gent
At a bazaar
Paid for
A kiss
But got a jar
Burma-Shave. (Verse 261)

The place to pass
On curves
You know
Is only at
A beauty show
Burma-Shave. (Verse 262)

Don't pass cars
On curve or hill
If the cops
Don't get you
Morticians will
Burma-Shave. (Verse 263)

Sleep in a chair
Nothing to lose
But a nap
At the wheel
Is a permanent snooze
Burma-Shave. (Verse 264)

No lady likes
To dance
Or dine
Accompanied by
A porcupine
Burma-Shave. (Verse 265)

When you lay
Those few cents down
You've bought
The smoothest
Shave in town
Burma-Shave. (Verse 266)

Leap year's over
You're safe, men
All you cowards
Can shave again
With brushless
Burma-Shave. (Verse 267)

Men
With whiskers
'Neath their noses
Oughta have to kiss
Like Eskimoses
Burma-Shave. (Verse 268)

Rip Van Winkle
Said he'd rather
Snooze for years
Than shave
With lather
Burma-Shave. (Verse 269)

Pa acted
So tickled
Ma thot
He was pickled
He'd just tried
Burma-Shave. (Verse 270)

One pound jar 85¢
Half pound jar 50¢
Big tube 35¢
Don't put it off
Put it on
Burma-Shave. (Verse 271)

The bearded devil
Is forced
To dwell
In the only place
Where they don't sell
Burma-Shave. (Verse 272)

Altho insured
Remember, kiddo
They don't pay you
They pay
Your widow
Burma-Shave. (Verse 273)

It gave
McDonald
That needed charm
Hello Hollywood
Good-by farm
Burma-Shave. (Verse 274)

My job is
Keeping faces clean
And nobody knows
De stubble
I've seen
Burma-Shave. (Verse 275)

Dear lover boy,
Your photo came
But your doggone beard
Won't fit
The frame
Burma-Shave. (Verse 276)

Take
Your
Time
Not
Your life
Burma-Shave. (Verse 277)

Ashes to ashes
Forests to dust
Keep Wisconsin green
Or we'll
All go bust
Burma-Shave. (Verse 278)

Feel your face
As you ride by
Now don't
You think
It's time to try
Burma-Shave. (Verse 279)

Drove too long
Driver snoozing
What happened next
Is not
Amusing
Burma-Shave. (Verse 280)

Many a wolf
Is never let in
Because of the hair
On his
Chinny-chin-chin
Burma-Shave. (Verse 281)

Fire! Fire!
Keep cool
Be brave
Just grab
Your pants and
Burma-Shave. (Verse 282)

One pound 85 cents
Half pound 50 cents
Big tube 35 cents
Don't put it off
Put it on
Burma-Shave. (Verse 283)

He always used
A steaming towel
And mug and brush
And language foul
'Til he tried
Burma-Shave. (Verse 284)

Several million
Modern men
Will never
Go back
To the brush again
Burma-Shave. (Verse 285)

A beard
That's rough
And overgrown
is better than
A chaperone
Burma-Shave. (Verse 286)

Tho tough
And rough
From wind and wave
Your cheek grows sleek
With
Burma-Shave. (Verse 287)

First men buy it
Then apply it
Then advise
Their friends
To try it
Burma-Shave. (Verse 288)

What you shouted
May be true,
But
Did you hear
What he called you?
Burma-Shave. (Verse 289)

Tell
The dear
Who shops around
That half a buck
Buys half a pound
Burma-Shave. (Verse 290)

Gets each
Whisker
At the base
No ingrown hair
On neck or face
Burma-Shave. (Verse 291)

Famous last words
"If he won't
Dim his
I won't
Dim mine"
Burma-Shave. (Verse 292)

When the stork
Delivers a boy
Our whole
Darn factory
Jumps for joy
Burma-Shave. (Verse 293)

When junior takes
Your ties
And car
It's time to buy
An extra jar
Burma-Shave. (Verse 294)

Use our cream
And we betcha
Girls won't wait
They'll come
And getcha
Burma-Shave. (Verse 295)

Big blue tube
It's a honey
Best squeeze play
For love
Or money
Burma-Shave. (Verse 296)

Our fortune
Is your
Shaven face
It's our best
Advertising space
Burma-Shave. (Verse 297)

Soaps
That irritate
Their mugs
Turn jolly gents
To jitterbugs
Burma-Shave. (Verse 298)

No use
Knowing
How to pick 'em
If your half-shaved
Whiskers stick 'em
Burma-Shave. (Verse 299)

Shaving brushes
You'll soon see 'em
Way down east
In some
Museum
Burma-Shave. (Verse 300)

Prize contest details
May be obtained
At football broadcast
Every Saturday
Over WCCO
Burma-Shave. (Verse 301)

If substitution
He should try
Just look that clerk
Right in the eye
And bellow
Burma-Shave. (Verse 302)

He had the ring
He had the flat
But she felt his chin
And that
Was that
Burma-Shave. (Verse 303)

Free
Illustrated
Jingle book
In every
Package
Burma-Shave. (Verse 304)

Little shavers
Don't overlook
Illustrated
Jingle book
In every package
Burma-Shave. (Verse 305)

Mirror on
The bathroom wall
What's the
Smoothest shave
Of all?
Burma-Shave. (Verse 306)

Week-old beard
So masked his face
His bull dog
Chased him
Off the place
Burma-Shave. (Verse 307)

Shaving brush
All wet
And hairy
I've passed you up
For sanitary
Burma-Shave. (Verse 308)

Drive like
A railroad engineer
Take it easy
When the road's
Not clear
Burma-Shave. (Verse 309)

25 prizes
Every week
Thruout the football season
You'll find you'd rather
Use no lather
B'golly there's a reason
Burma-Shave. (Verse 310)

After one trial
You'll want more
At the next
Good drug store
15 for 25 cents
Burma-Shave Blades. (Verse 311)

Whiskers
Easy come
You know
Why not make them
Easy go?
Burma-Shave. (Verse 312)

Burma-Shave
Was such a boom
They passed
The bride
And kissed the groom
Burma-Shave. (Verse 313)

Unless
Your face
Is stinger free
You'd better let
Your honey be
Burma-Shave. (Verse 314)

Proper
Distance
To him was bunk
They pulled him out
Of some guy's trunk
Burma Shave. (Verse 315)

The monkey took
One look at Jim
And threw the peanut
Back at him
He needed
Burma-Shave. (Verse 316)

The blackened forest
Smoulders yet
Because
He flipped
A cigaret
Burma-Shave. (Verse 317)

The one who
Drives when
He's been drinking
Depends on you
To do his thinking
Burma-Shave. (Verse 318)

Drinking drivers
Enhance their
Chance
To highball home
In an ambulance
Burma-Shave. (Verse 319)

All little rhyming
Jokes aside
Don't be content
Until you've
Tried
Burma-Shave. (Verse 320)

Buy a jar
Take it from me
There's so
Much in it
The last half's free
Burma-Shave. (Verse 321)

A guy
Who drives
A car wide open
Is not thinkin'
He's just hopin'
Burma-Shave. (Verse 322)

Ring out the old
Ring in the new
What good can
Shaving
Brushes do?
Burma-Shave. (Verse 323)

Jar so big
Cost so small
Coolest
Smoothest
Shave of all
Burma-Shave. (Verse 324)

Drinking drivers-
Nothing worse
They put
The quart
Before the hearse
Burma-Shave. (Verse 325)

Car in ditch
Driver in tree
Moon was full
And so
Was he
Burma-Shave. (Verse 326)

The wolf
Who longs
To roam and prowl
Should shave before
He starts to howl
Burma-Shave. (Verse 327)

A big
Improvement
Since the war
Is now on sale
In your drug store
Burma-Shave.
No price increase. (Verse 328)

His rose
is wed
His violet blew
But his sugar is sweet
Since he took this cue
Burma-Shave. (Verse 329)

At Xmas time
And birthdays too
We solve
Your problems right
For you—give
Burma-Shave. (Verse 330)

A scratchy chin
Like bright
Pink socks
Puts any romance
On the rocks
Burma-Shave. (Verse 331)

We've made
Grandpa
Look so trim
The local
Draft board's after him
Burma-Shave. (Verse 332)

It took years
To perfect
For you
A brushless cream
That's greaseless too
Burma-Shave. (Verse 333)

A Christmas hug
A birthday kiss
Awaits
The woman
Who gives this
Burma-Shave. (Verse 334)

Altho
We've sold
Six million others
We still can't sell
Those coughdrop brothers
Burma-Shave. (Verse 335)

No soggy brushes
In your grip
You've always
Got a
Finger tip
Burma-Shave. (Verse 336)

Grandpa's
Out with
Junior's date
Old technique
With brand new bait
Burma-Shave. (Verse 337)

Missin'
Kissin'?
Perhaps your thrush
Can't get thru
The underbrush—try
Burma-Shave. (Verse 338)

The safest rule
No ifs or buts
Just drive
Like every one else
Is nuts!
Burma-Shave. (Verse 339)

Stores are full
Of shaving aids
But all you need
Is this
And blades
Burma-Shave. (Verse 340)

Mom and Pop
Are feeling gay
Baby said
As plain
As day
Burma-Shave. (Verse 341)

If a gift
You must choose
Give him
One that
He can use
Burma-Shave. (Verse 342)

There's no whisker
it won't soften
Shave 'em close
And not
So often
Burma-Shave. (Verse 343)

Traveling men
Know ease
And speed
Their shaving kits
Hold what they need
Burma-Shave. (Verse 344)

No pulling
At the whisker base
A soothing film
Protects
Your face
Burma-Shave. (Verse 345)

On curves ahead
Remember, sonny
That rabbit's foot
Didn't save
The bunny
Burma-Shave. (Verse 346)

"My cheek"
Says she
"Feels smooth as satin"
"Ha! Ha!" Says he
"That's mine you're pattin'"
Burma-Shave. (Verse 347)

Soap
May do
For lads with fuzz
Bur sir, you ain't
The kid you wuz
Burma-Shave. (Verse 348)

He tried
To cross
As fast train neared
Death didn't draft him
He volunteered
Burma-Shave. (Verse 349)

The Burma girls
In Mandalay
Dunk bearded lovers
In the bay
Who don't use
Burma-Shave. (Verse 350)

If you think
She likes
Your bristles
Walk bare-footed
Through some thistles
Burma-Shave. (Verse 351)

Wild men pulled
Their whiskers out
That's what made
Them wild
No doubt—
Burma-Shave. (Verse 352)

It's in
The bag
Of every man
Who travels
Lightly as he can
Burma-Shave. (Verse 353)

I use it too
The bald man said
It keeps my face
Just like
My head
Burma-Shave. (Verse 354)

The crowd
You see
Around that store
Are Burma-Shavers
Buying more
Burma-Shave. (Verse 355)

If you want
A hearty squeeze
Get our
Female
Anti-freeze
Burma-Shave. (Verse 356)

You can beat
A mile a minute
But there ain't
No future
In it
Burma-Shave. (Verse 357)

156

Buying defense bonds
Means money lent
So they
Don't cost you
One red cent
Burma-Shave. (Verse 358)

Rhyme and reason
Every season
You've read
The rhyme
Now try the reason
Burma-Shave. (Verse 359)

Dewhiskered
Kisses
Defrost
The
Misses
Burma-Shave. (Verse 360)

Everything
In it
Is fine
For the
Skin
Burma-Shave. (Verse 361)

Shiver my timbers
Said Captain Mack
We're ten knots out
But we're turning back
I forgot my
Burma-Shave. (Verse 362)

Take a tip
For your trip
No wet brush
To soak
Your grip
Burma-Shave. (Verse 363)

If man bites doggie
That is news
If face
Scares doggie
Better use
Burma-Shave. (Verse 364)

Always remember
On any trip
Keep two things
Within your grip
Your steering wheel and
Burma-Shave. (Verse 365)

That "pink toothbrush"
Is a curse
But that pink razor's
A darn sight worse
Use
Burma-Shave. (Verse 366)

It's not toasted
It's not dated
But look out—
It's imitated
Insist on
Burma-Shave. (Verse 367)

Hit 'em high
Hit 'em low
Follow your team
Over WCCO
And win a prize
Burma-Shave. (Verse 368)

Hit 'em high
Hit 'em low
It's action rooters crave
Millions boast—millions toast
The All-American shave
Burma-Shave. (Verse 369)

Give the guy
The toe of your boot
Who tries
To hand you
A substitute for
Burma-Shave. (Verse 370)

Substitutes
Would irk a saint
You hope they are
What you know
They ain't
Burma-Shave. (Verse 371)

Drinking drivers
Don't you know
Great bangs
From little
Binges grow?
Burma-Shave. (Verse 372)

Prices rising
O'er the nation
Here is one
That missed
Inflation
Burma-Shave. (Verse 373)

If your hubby
Trumps your ace
Here's something
That will
Save his face
Burma-Shave. (Verse 374)

The tube's
A whopper
35 cents
Easy shaving
Low expense
Burma-Shave. (Verse 375)

His face was smooth
And cool as ice
And oh Louise!
He smelled
So nice
Burma-Shave. (Verse 376)

With 200 kinds
From which to choose
2 million men
Prefer
To use
Burma-Shave. (Verse 377)

158

Congressman Pipp
Lost the election
Babies he kissed
Had no protection
To win—use
Burma-Shave. (Verse 378)

Soldier
Sailor
And marine
Now get a shave
That's quick and clean
Burma-Shave. (Verse 379)

She raised cain
When he raised stubble
Guess what
Smoothed away
Their trouble?
Burma-Shave. (Verse 380)

Careless driving
Soon we hope
Will go
The way
Of brush and soap
Burma-Shave. (Verse 381)

Life is sweet
But oh how bitter!
To love a gal
And then
Not git 'er
Burma-Shave. (Verse 382)

Better try
Less speed per mile
That car
May have to
Last a while
Burma-Shave. (Verse 383)

Violets are blue
Roses are pink
On graves
Of those
Who drive and drink
Burma-Shave. (Verse 384)

That barefoot
Chap
With cheeks of tan
Won't let 'em chap
When he's a man
Burma-Shave. (Verse 385)

I know
He's a wolf
Said riding hood
But Grandma dear,
He smells so good
Burma-Shave. (Verse 386)

This cream
Makes the
Gardener's daughter
Plant her tu-lips
Where she oughter
Burma-Shave. (Verse 387)

Relief
For faces
Chapped and sore
Keeps 'em comin'
Back for more
Burma-Shave. (Verse 388)

If you dislike
Big traffic fines
Slow down
'Till you
Can read these signs
Burma-Shave. (Verse 389)

Why is it
When you
Try to pass
The guy in front
Goes twice as fast?
Burma-Shave. (Verse 390)

A silky cheek
Shaved smooth
And clean
Is not obtained
With a mowing machine
Burma-Shave. (Verse 391)

If anything
Will please
Your Jill
A little jack
For this jar will
Burma-Shave. (Verse 392)

These signs
Are not
For laughs alone
The face they save
May be your own
Burma-Shave. (Verse 393)

To change that
Shaving job
To joy
You gotta use
The real McCoy
Burma-Shave. (Verse 394)

Baby your skin
Keep it fitter
Or "baby"
Will get
Another sitter
Burma-Shave. (Verse 395)

Prickly pears
Are picked
For pickles
No peach picks
A face that prickles
Burma-Shave. (Verse 396)

In Cupid's little
Bag of trix
Here's the one
That clix
With chix
Burma-Shave. (Verse 397)

Man passes
Dog house
Dog sees chin
Dog gets out
Man gets in
Burma-Shave. (Verse 398)

We know
How much
You love that gal
But use both hands
For driving, pal
Burma-Shave. (Verse 399)

Travelers
All
You need is
A razor
And
Burma-Shave. (Verse 400)

A shave
That's real
No cuts to heal
A soothing
Velvet after-feel
Burma-Shave. (Verse 401)

A peach
Looks good
With lots of fuzz
But man's no peach
And never wuz
Burma-Shave. (Verse 402)

The bearded lady
Tried a jar
She's now
A famous
Movie star
Burma-Shave. (Verse 403)

Film protects
Your neck
And chin
So your razor
Won't dig in
Burma-Shave. (Verse 404)

Try a tube
The cream
That's in it
Is making friends
A man a minute
Burma-Shave. (Verse 405)

Can't shave daily?
Tender hide?
Now be honest
Have you
Tried
Burma-Shave. (Verse 406)

Six
Hundred
Thousand
Men
Use
Burma-Shave. (Verse 407)

Guys whose eyes
Are in
Their backs
Get halos crossing
Railroad tracks
Burma-Shave. (Verse 408)

Half a pound
For
Half a buck
Come on shavers
You're in luck
Burma-Shave. (Verse 409)

Hello druggist
I don't mean maybe
Yes
Sir.
That's the baby
Burma-Shave. (Verse 410)

Half a buck
Half a pound
No substitute
Is ever found
For
Burma-Shave. (Verse 411)

Hat and tie
Smart and clean
Space between
Spoiled the scene
He should use
Burma-Shave. (Verse 412)

A guy
Who wants
To middle-aisle it
Must never scratch
His little violet
Burma-Shave. (Verse 413)

If you're just
An average man
Wanting to look
The best you can
Use
Burma-Shave. (Verse 414)

Shaving brushes
Soon will
Be trimmin'
Those screwy hats
We see on wimmin
Burma-Shave. (Verse 415)

Its not
How fast or slow
You drive
The question is
How you arrive
Burma-Shave. (Verse 416)

Enthusiastic user
Henry J. McLass
Spreads our product
On the lawn
When he cuts the grass
Burma-Shave. (Verse 417)

Pat's bristles
Scratched
Bridget's nose
That's when
Her wild Irish rose
Burma-Shave. (Verse 418)

Are you
An even-tempered guy
Mad all
The time?
Better try
Burma-Shave. (Verse 419)

Smith Brothers
Would look immense
If they'd just
Cough up 50 cents
For half pound jar
Burma-Shave. (Verse 420)

If HER whiskers
Scratched YOUR cheek
You would
Send her out
To seek
Burma-Shave. (Verse 421)

The cream
Preserves
Pa's razor blade
The jar preserves
Ma's marmalade
Burma-Shave. (Verse 422)

They missed
The turn
Car was whizz'n
Fault was her'n
Funeral his'n
Burma-Shave. (Verse 423)

We can't
Provide you
With a date
But we do supply
The best darn bait
Burma-Shave. (Verse 424)

Clancy's
Whiskers
Tickled Nancy
Nancy lowered the boom
On Clancy!
Burma-Shave. (Verse 425)

Golfers
If fewer strokes
Are what you crave
You're out of the rough
With
Burma-Shave. (Verse 426)

I'd heard
It praised
By drug store clerks
I tried the stuff
Hot dog! It works
Burma-Shave. (Verse 427)

163

His crop of
Whiskers
Needed reaping
That's what kept
His Lena leaping
Burma-Shave. (Verse 428)

Substitutes!
Smooth guys sell 'em
Easy marks use 'em
Well groomed men
Always refuse 'em
Burma-Shave. (Verse 429)

Makes shaving
A
Grin game
Not
A skin game
Burma-Shave. (Verse 430)

Jonah took
No brush
To mop his face
Where Jonah went
He needed space
Burma-Shave. (Verse 431)

Special seats
Reserved in hades
For whiskered guys
Who scratch
The ladies
Burma-Shave. (Verse 432)

Mug and brush
Old Adam
Had 'em
Is your husband
Like Adam, Madam?
Burma-Shave. (Verse 433)

Substitutes
Like unseen barter
Often make one
Sad
But smarter
Burma-Shave. (Verse 434)

You'll love your wife
You'll love her paw
You'll even love
Your mother-in-law
If you use
Burma-Shave. (Verse 435)

Every second
Without fail
Some store
Rings up
Another sale
Burma-Shave. (Verse 436)

Shaving brush
In army pack
Was straw that broke
The rookie's back
Use brushless
Burma-Shave. (Verse 437)

164

Both hands
On wheel
Eyes on road
That's the skillful
Driver's code
Burma-Shave. (Verse 438)

He used
Umbrella
For parachute
Now rejects
Every substitute
Burma-Shave. (Verse 439)

On a highway ad
He spied it
Bought a jar
Now glad he
Tried it
Burma-Shave. (Verse 440)

Christmas comes
But once
A year
One swell gift
That's always here
Burma-Shave. (Verse 441)

Her chariot
Raced 80 per
They hauled away
What had
Ben Hur
Burma-Shave. (Verse 442)

No matter
The price
No matter how new
The best safety device
In your car is you
Burma-Shave. (Verse 443)

These signs
We gladly
Dedicate
To men who've had
No date of late
Burma-Shave. (Verse 444)

Headline news
For face
And chin
Now improved
With lanolin
Burma-Shave. (Verse 445)

Pull off
The road
To change a flat
Protect your life—
No spare for that!
Burma-Shave. (Verse 446)

Substitutes
Can do
More harm
Than city fellers
On a farm
Burma-Shave. (Verse 447)

The boy who gets
His girl's applause
Must act
Not look
Like Santa Claus
Burma-Shave. (Verse 448)

Every shaver
Now can snore
Six more minutes
Than before
By using
Burma-Shave. (Verse 449)

At crossroads
Don't just
Trust to luck
The other car
May be a truck
Burma-Shave. (Verse 450)

"It's off!"
He cried
And felt his chin
'Twas just another
Easy win for
Burma-Shave. (Verse 451)

At school zones
Heed instructions
Protect
Our little
Tax deductions
Burma-Shave. (Verse 452)

We're widely read
And often quoted
But it's shaves
Not signs
For which we're noted
Burma-Shave. (Verse 453)

No man can really
Do his stuff
With a face that's sore
Or a chin
That's rough
Burma-Shave. (Verse 454)

This will never
Come to pass
A back-seat
Driver
Out of gas
Burma-Shave. (Verse 455)

College cutie
Pigskin hero
Bristly Kiss
Hero
Zero
Burma-Shave. (Verse 456)

Drowsy?
Just remember, pard
That marble slab
Is doggone
Hard
Burma-Shave. (Verse 457)

The big blue tube's
Just like Louise
You get
A thrill
From every squeeze
Burma-Shave. (Verse 458)

Try a tube
Its cooling
Power
Refreshes like
An April shower
Burma-Shave. (Verse 459)

The answer to
A maiden's prayer
Is a man
Most anywhere
Using
Burma-Shave. (Verse 460)

For shaving comfort
Without
A sting
That big blue tube
Has everything
Burma-Shave. (Verse 461)

Substitutes
Resemble
Tail-chasing pup
Follow and follow
But never catch up
Burma-Shave. (Verse 462)

His tenor voice
She thought divine
Till whiskers
Scratched
Sweet Adeline
Burma-Shave. (Verse 463)

Old McDonald
On the farm
Shaved so hard
He broke his arm
Then he bought
Burma-Shave. (Verse 464)

Darling I am
Growing old
Nonsense!
Do as you
Are told—get
Burma-Shave. (Verse 465)

These three
Prevent most accidents
Courtesy
Caution
Common sense
Burma-Shave. (Verse 466)

Tube immense
Still
35 cents
Easy shaving
Low expense
Burma-Shave.
No price increase. (Verse 467)

Substitutes
Are like a girdle
They find some jobs
They just
Can't hurdle
Burma-Shave. (Verse 468)

It spreads so smooth
It shaves so slick
It feels
Like velvet
And it's quick
Burma-Shave. (Verse 469)

Of all
The drunks
Who drive on Sunday
Some are still
Alive on Monday
Burma-Shave. (Verse 470)

From statistics
That we gather
The swing is to
No brush
No lather
Burma-Shave. (Verse 471)

Paper hangers
With the hives
Now can
Shave with
Carving knives
Burma-Shave. (Verse 472)

Life with father
Is more pleasant
Since
He got this
Birthday present
Burma-Shave. (Verse 473)

Others claim
Their product good
But ours
Does what
You think it should
Burma-Shave. (Verse 474)

Men who
Have to
Travel light
Find the 35 cent tube
Just right
Burma-Shave. (Verse 475)

Bristles scratched
His cookie's map
That's what
Made poor
Ginger snap
Burma-Shave. (Verse 476)

Your razor
Floats thru
The hair
With the
Greatest of ease
Burma-Shave. (Verse 477)

His beard
Was long
And strong and tough
He lost his
Chicken in the rough
Burma-Shave. (Verse 478)

Does your husband
Misbehave
Grunt and grumble
Rant and rave
Shoot the brute some
Burma-Shave. (Verse 479)

Wise old Sandy
Shopped around
This is what
Old Sandy found
50 cents buys half a pound
Burma-Shave. (Verse 480)

When you drive
If caution ceases
You are apt
To rest
In pieces
Burma-Shave. (Verse 481)

Men
Who've tested
Every brand
Are just the ones
Who now demand
Burma-Shave. (Verse 482)

The queen
Of hearts
Now loves the knave
The king
Ran out of
Burma-Shave. (Verse 483)

Leaves
Face soft
As woman's touch
Yet doesn't cost you
Near as much
Burma-Shave. (Verse 484)

Passing cars
When you can't see
May get you
A glimpse
Of eternity
Burma-Shave. (Verse 485)

To soothe
And smooth
Your tender skin
It's now improved
With lanolin
Burma-Shave. (Verse 486)

If a gift
You must choose
Give him one
He'll like
To use
Burma-Shave. (Verse 487)

To steal
A kiss
He had the knack
But lacked the cheek
To get one back
Burma-Shave. (Verse 488)

His brush
Is gone
So what'll we do
Said Mike Robe I
To Mike Robe II
Burma-Shave. (Verse 489)

He's the boy
The gals forgot
His line
Was smooth
His chin was not
Burma-Shave. (Verse 490)

Pa likes the cream
Ma likes the jar
Both like
The price
So there you are
Burma-Shave. (Verse 491)

"No, no,"
She said
To her bristly beau
"I'd rather
Eat the mistletoe"
Burma-Shave. (Verse 492)

Cattle crossing
Means go slow
That old bull
Is some
Cow's beau
Burma-Shave. (Verse 493)

Don't leave safety
To mere chance
That's why
Belts are
Sold with pants
Burma-Shave. (Verse 494)

Forest fires
Start from scratch
So think before
You toss
That match.
Burma-Shave. (Verse 495)

"One Burma-Shave,"
The school boy cried
"At least
I'll smell
As if I tried"
Burma-Shave. (Verse 496)

The wife
Who keeps on
Being kissed
Always heads
Her shopping list
Burma-Shave. (Verse 497)

The wolf
Is shaved
So neat and trim
Red Riding Hood
Is chasing him
Burma-Shave. (Verse 498)

In every
Half a pound
My boy
You get a ton
Of shaving joy
Burma-Shave. (Verse 499)

Bachelor's quarters
Dog on the rug
Whiskers to blame
No one
To hug
Burma-Shave. (Verse 500)

'Mid rising
Taxes
Soaring rents
Still half a pound
For fifty cents
Burma-Shave. (Verse 501)

The 50 cent jar
So large
By heck
Even the Scotch
Now shave the neck
Burma-Shave. (Verse 502)

Holler!
Half a pound
For half a dollar
Isn't that
A cheerful earful?
Burma-Shave. (Verse 503)

Fingers were made
Before brushes—
Use 'em
They're much safer
You can't lose 'em
Burma-Shave. (Verse 504)

Hear about
The jolly tar
It smelled so good
He ate
A jar
Burma-Shave. (Verse 505)

Spread it on
And lightly too
Shave it off
That's all
You're through
Burma-Shave. (Verse 506)

Salesmen, tourists
Camper-outers
All you other
Whisker-sprouters
Don't forget your
Burma-Shave. (Verse 507)

_____(Hebrew)
_____(Chinese)
_____(Greek)
The best shave
In any language
Burma-Shave. (Verse (508)

Tho tough
And rough
From wind and wave
Your cheek grows sleek
With
Burma-Shave. (Verse 509)

Beneath
This stone
Lies Elmer Gush
Tickled to death
By his shaving brush
Burma-Shave. (Verse 510)

20 miles per gal.
Says well-known car
To go 10,000
Miles per gal
By half-pound jar
Burma-Shave. (Verse 511)

Cheer cheer
The gang's
All here
Riding along
Three million strong for
Burma-Shave. (Verse 512)

Regardless of
Political views
All good parties
Always
Choose
Burma-Shave. (Verse 513)

His line was smooth
But not his chin
He took her out
She took him in
To buy some
Burma-Shave. (Verse 514)

Look
Don't listen
Pop is trying
A substitute
Instead of buying
Burma-Shave. (Verse 515)

Substitutes
That promise perfection
Are like
Some candidates
After election
Burma-Shave. (Verse 516)

Wild
Dashes
From by-ways
Cause crashes
On highways
Burma-Shave. (Verse 517)

"At ease" she said
"Maneuvers begin
When you get
Those whiskers
Off your chin"
Burma-Shave. (Verse 518)

Special treatment
Every hair
Holds it up
And cuts
It square
Burma-Shave. (Verse 519)

Moonlight
And roses
Whiskers
Like Moses
Just don't go together
Burma-Shave. (Verse 520)

Ruddy cheeks
And face
Of tan
Neatly shaven
What a man
Burma-Shave. (Verse 521)

Bathroom shelf
Surprises me
From shaving clutter
It's now free
I'm using
Burma-Shave. (Verse 522)

Thrifty shavers
Now are found
Buying shaves
By the pound
One lb. jar 85 cents
Burma-Shave. (Verse 523)

Give hand signals
To those behind
They don't know
What's in
Your mind
Burma-Shave. (Verse 524)

Lawyers, doctors
Sheiks and bakers
Mountaineers and undertakers
Make their bristly beards behave
By using brushless
Burma-Shave. (Verse 525)

When Peter Piper
Pickle picker
Kissed his gal
His beard
Would prick 'er
Burma-Shave. (Verse 526)

It gave
Swell shaves before
Now you'll like it
Even more
The new—improved
Burma-Shave. (Verse 527)

Political pull
May be
Of use
For razor pull
There's no excuse
Burma-Shave. (Verse 528)

At a quiz
Pa ain't
No whiz
But he knows how
To keep Ma his
Burma-Shave. (Verse 529)

Every day
We do
Our part
To make your face
A work of art
Burma-Shave. (Verse 530)

My neck was sore
In front before
And also
Sore behind
Before
Burma-Shave. (Verse 531)

Careless
Bridegroom
Dainty bride
Scratchy whiskers
Homicide
Burma-Shave. (Verse 532)

Tube
Immense
35 cents
Easy shaving
Low expense
Burma-Shave. (Verse 533)

Whiskers long
Made Samson strong
But Samson's gal
She done
Him wrong
Burma-Shave. (Verse 534)

Substitutes would
Have their place
If you could
Substitute
Your face
Burma-Shave. (Verse 535)

She eyed
His beard
And said no dice
The wedding's off-
I'll COOK the rice
Burma-Shave. (Verse 536)

Before I tried it
The kisses
I missed
But afterward — Boy!
The misses I kissed
Burma-Shave. (Verse 537)

His face
Was loved
By just his mother
He Burma-Shaved
And now—
Oh, brother. (Verse 538)

To most brush shavers
It's quite clear
The yanks aren't coming
The yanks are here
Use brushless
Burma-Shave. (Verse 539)

You've laughed
At our signs
For many a mile
Be a sport
Give us a trial
Burma-Shave. (Verse 540)

Is he
Lonesome
Or just blind—
This guy who drives
So close behind?
Burma-Shave. (Verse 541)

Avoid the store
Which claims
You should
Buy something else
That's just as good
Burma-Shave. (Verse 542)

Many a forest
Used to stand
Where a
Lighted match
Got out of hand
Burma-Shave. (Verse 543)

This cream
Is like
A parachute
There isn't
Any substitute
Burma-Shave. (Verse 544)

To a substitute
He gave a trial
It took off
Nothing
But his smile
Burma-Shave. (Verse 545)

Use this cream
A day
Or two
Then don't call her-
She'll call you
Burma-Shave. (Verse 546)

Highways are
No place
To sleep
Stop your car
To count your sheep
Burma-Shave. (Verse 547)

If you
Must sample
Her "pucker paint"
Better drive
Where traffic ain't
Burma-Shave. (Verse 548)

The cream
One hears
The most of now
Comes from a jar
Not from a cow
Burma-Shave. (Verse 549)

Hinky-dinky
Parley voo
Cheer up face
The war
Is thru
Burma-Shave. (Verse 550)

Eight
Hundred
Thousand
Men
Use
Burma-Shave. (Verse 551)

The cannoneers
With hairy ears
On wiry whiskers
Used tin shears
Until they found
Burma-Shave. (Verse 552)

1880 AD.
Straight razor and
Shaving soap
1930 AD.
Safety razor and
Burma-Shave. (Verse 553)

If daisies
Are your
Favorite flower
Keep pushin' up those
Miles-per-hour
Burma-Shave. (Verse 554)

Early to bed
Early to rise
Was meant for those
Old fashioned guys
Who didn't use
Burma-Shave. (Verse 555)

The whale
Put Jonah
Down the hatch
But coughed him up
Because he scratched
Burma-Shave. (Verse 556)

MAJOR WORD INDEX
TO BURMA-SHAVE RHYMES

177

179

million, 227
millions, 138
minute, 357
minutes, 9, 449
mirror, 244, 306
misbehave, 28, 479
misfortune, 137
miss, 164
misses, 360, 537
mistake, 39
mistakes, 200
mistletoe, 492
modern, 3, 4, 10, 14,
    155, 229
moisten, 241
mom, 341
Monday, 470
money, 5, 225, 296
monkey, 316
moonlight, 520
mop, 431
more, 311
morning, 35
morticians, 263
Moses, 520
mother, 538
mother-in-law, 435
mountaineers, 525
movie, 403
mow, 208
mowing, 391
Mrs., 142
mug, 222, 284
mugs, 298
multitude, 126

muscle, 49
museum, 11, 300
mushy, 54
Nancy, 425
nature, 198
naughty, 111
neck, 404, 502
needed, 274
neophyte, 86
nerve, 68
nerves, 18
New York, 230
nice, 376
nix, 143
no ma'ams, 85
Noah, 103
nowadays, 149
nudist, 110
nurse, 35
nuts, 339
ocean, 183
off, 128
offender, 218
offered, 227
often, 343
old-fashion, 555
on, 2
oncoming, 30
one-horse, 97
onions, 189
over-ripe, 54
overgrown, 286
pa, 270
pain, 76
paint, 548

painting, 98
palms, 251
pants, 282, 494
paper, 472
parachute, 439, 544
parley voo, 550
pass, 263, 390
passing, 214
past, 13
pats, 229
Paul, 44, 114
paw, 435
peach, 65, 396, 402
peanut, 316
Pedro, 253
Pentagon, 168
pep, 184
perfect, 333
periscope, 214
permanent, 264
Peter Piper, 526
photo, 276
picked, 396
picker, 526
pickle, 526
pickled, 270
pickles, 396
pieces, 481
pigskin, 456
pike, 107
pink, 331, 366
pipp, 378
pity, 190
place, 307
places, 132

violets, 384
voice, 463
volunteered, 349
wake, 15
wall, 306
war, 6, 13, 236, 328, 550
wash, 14
water, 194
wave, 287
way, 4
WCCO, 301
weather, 237
wed, 329
week, 48, 225
week-old, 307
whale, 556
what fur, 55
wheel, 365
whiff, 185
whisker, 190, 194, 343, 345
whiskered, 249, 261
whiskers, 15, 17, 50, 79, 162, 208, 233, 312, 425, 520, 552
whiskery, 205
whiskey, 45
whistle, 62, 254
whiz, 529
whizz'n, 423
whoop, 52
whopper, 375
widder, 211
wide open, 322
widow, 36, 273

wife, 223, 249
wild, 260, 352
wild Irish, 418
Willie, 113
willin', 209
wilter, 194
wimmin', 415
wind, 287
winkle, 269
wiry, 552
wives, 121
wolf, 281, 327, 386, 498
woman, 334, 484
wood, 227
woolly, 260
work of art, 530
worse, 89, 325
wrecked, 248
wrecks, 207
x, 237
Xmas, 330
yanks, 539
years, 241
younger, 7
youth, 38
zero, 456
zip, 202
zipper, 202
zones, 452

Bill Vossler likes to remember the best of the past, like Burma-Shave signs, which is why he chose to use a fifteen-year-old photo of himself. Vossler, a full-time writer with more than 2,200 articles to his credit published in 150 magazines, lives with his wife, Nikki Rajala, and their two cats, Mittens and Dynamo, in Rockville, Minnesota. Vossler's first book, *Orphan Tractors*, published by Motorbooks International, appeared in August 1996.

188